Three Sisters

ANTON CHEKHOV

Three Sisters

TRANSLATED BY PAUL SCHMIDT

TCG TRANSLATIONS

1992

Chekhov, Anton Pavlovich, 1860-1904.
 [Tri sestry. English]
 Three sisters / Anton Chekhov ; translated by Paul Schmidt.—1st ed.
 (TCG Translations 3)
 Translation of: Tri sestry.
 ISBN 1-55936-056-9 (cloth)—ISBN 1-55936-055-0 (paper)
 I. Schmidt, Paul, 1934-   II. Title.   III. Series
 PG3456.T8S35 1992
891.72'3—dc20   92-11369
                                                                            CIP

Cover design and watercolor copyright (c) 1992 by Barry Moser
Design and composition by The Sarabande Press
Color separations provided by EMR Systems Communication

First Edition, September 1992
Second Printing, March 2000

CONTENTS

Introduction

I knew this book needed an introduction when someone asked me, with a sigh, why make yet another English translation of Chekhov's *Three Sisters*? But this is another American translation, not another English translation.

I believe it's crucial to make the distinction. We tend to think we and the Britons share a common tongue, but in the theatre, where language as it is spoken is paramount, it's always clear that we speak two different dialects, mutually understandable, true, but each with its own accents, idioms and emotive speech rhythms. For a long time we relied on British translations of Chekhov, and so we tended to think he spoke the language of Shaw and Galsworthy, and we tended to equate his characters with theirs. What Chekhov created belongs in fact to a very different world.

I believe, too, that most theatre texts need continual re-translating. While the language of the original remains fixed in time, the language of every audience changes enough in forty or fifty years to make a new translation necessary. And faster even than language, theatrical sensibilities change. The "skies of gray" that Gershwin found in Chekhov productions in the

Twenties have cleared a little; the "moody Russian soul" our parents went to Chekhov to observe turns out to be remarkably like our own. And we in America no longer admire the autumnal melancholy, the wistful nostalgia for gentility that so many English productions have laid upon Chekhov's plays.

A particular reason for me to translate the play is that I am a playwright and actor who happens to be a Russian scholar. Most of the published translations of Chekhov are done either by native Russians, whose English is often awkward and stilted, or by Russian scholars, whose English is often formal and unidiomatic. The others are "versions" or "adaptations" done by playwrights who know no Russian; they work either by comparing existing translations, or by hiring a Russian to help them. Inevitably their sense of what Chekhov actually wrote is extremely attenuated. And when they are playwrights with a strong dramatic language of their own, Chekhov's style and nuance are usually subordinated to theirs.

Three Sisters was written in 1900. The central question for us today is, what kind of existence can it have after almost a hundred years, in a theatre that is radically different from the one that gave it birth? That was in fact the real stimulus for this translation. The Wooster Group, a theatre company whose work I very much admire, asked me to make it for them. Their intention was to take this "classic" text, and try to stage it without any reference to the century-old tradition of Stanislavskian acting that still hangs about it like a worn-out coat.

That made sense to me. Chekhov's plays have been so linked with Stanislavsky's ideas that they are too often seen merely as vehicles for actors; we regularly speak of so-and-so's Vanya, what's-her-name's Arkadina. And actors in fact generally prefer *The Seagull* and *Uncle Vanya*, where long speeches and emotional scenes give them a chance to show off, to *Three*

Sisters and *The Cherry Orchard*, where the actor's role is subordinate to the extraordinary dramaturgy that Chekhov invents. I first worked on the text of *Three Sisters* over thirty years ago, with Randall Jarrell; it was a translation commissioned by The Actors Studio, and directed on Broadway by Lee Strasberg. That production was long talked of as the great American attempt to immortalize Method acting, to conquer Stanislavsky on his own ground. And as I remember the production, it was indeed all about acting, the creation of emotions; the grand musical structure of the play was hardly apparent. But the precise intention of the Wooster Group was to articulate Chekhov's musical structure, and to make that the focus of their production. I found the idea exciting, and agreed to join them to play the role of Chebutykin. We have now played the piece, under the title *Brace Up!*, for almost three years in ten different cities throughout the world.

Another reason that compelled me to this translation was the experience over many years of having American actors ask me to explain certain curious expressions, certain odd foreign behaviors indulged in by Chekhov's characters. Especially, over and over, I was asked to explain the mysterious workings of the samovar they had inevitably to confront onstage. Now, when reading Chekhov's plays I have always been struck by the absolute *ordinariness* of his language, and by the humdrum everyday actions of his characters. His entire art is the creation of extraordinary human depths out of the surface banalities of everyday life. And it usually turned out that the curious expressions, the oddness and foreignness, the mysteries of the text that bothered my actor friends, were oddities of the translation they were reading. Over the years, unfortunately, these oddities were passed along in versions of the plays done by people who couldn't read Russian, because, as far as they could tell, that's the way Chekhov's characters talked. But with

the exception of those few characters whose speech is marked
by rural dialecticisms or by comic locutions, Chekhov's characters speak quite ordinary Russian. Even after a hundred
years, it seems remarkably simple, colloquial and accessible.
And Chekhov himself was well aware of this need for a natural
style. In a letter to a novice playwright, Chekhov advises him
to "avoid unnecessary filler words, you don't need them in a
play—for instance, the word 'that' in the sentence 'you know
that there's nothing for sale here.' Whenever you're writing
dialogue, be careful about those 'thats.'" I wanted to make a
translation for American actors in the kind of plain language
Chekhov actually wrote, one that might remove some of these
nonexistent problems.

I hope, too, that this text may help American actors and
directors of the play to move away from the "Russianness" of
Three Sisters, and toward its universal humanity. It had always
seemed to me there must have been in 1900 women living in
Nebraska, let's say, who longed to go back to Boston where
they'd been born and brought up. That connection is lost, or
somehow trivialized, whenever I see an American actress done
up as a Russian peasant shuffle across the stage carrying a
samovar. In Chekhov's time a samovar was as ordinary an item
of domestic life as a television is today. To bring one onstage,
fraught with symbolism and "Russianness," is to miss the
point and lose the focus of the play. The quaintness of it goes
against everything Chekhov as a dramatist was striving for.

I have included some notes to the text; I hope they help to
make things clear for the performers. This text is intended for
those I admire as much as Chekhov did: people who make
theatre because they love it.

—*Paul Schmidt*
New York
April, 1992

Three Sisters

CHARACTERS

Andréi Prózorov.

Ólga ⎫
Másha ⎬ his sisters.
Irína ⎭

Natásha, his fiancée, later his wife.

Kulýgin, Másha's husband, a high school teacher.

Vershínin, colonel, battery commander.

Baron Túzenbach, first lieutenant.

Solyóny, captain.

Chebutýkin, army doctor.

Fedótik, second lieutenant.

Róhde, second lieutenant.

Ferapónt, janitor at the County Council, an old man.

Anfísa, the Prozorovs' eighty-year-old nurse.

Act One

The Prózorov house. A big living room, separated by columns from a dining room in the rear. It is noon; the weather is sunny and bright. In the dining room the table is being set for lunch.

Ólga wears a dark blue high-school teacher's dress; she stands or walks about, correcting blue books. Másha wears a black dress; she is seated reading, with her hat on her lap. Irína wears a white dress; she stands lost in thought.

OLGA: It's a year ago today that father died, May fifth, on your birthday, Irína. It was very cold, and it snowed. I never thought I'd live through it. You fainted and you were lying there as if you were dead too. But now it's a year later and it doesn't bother us to talk about it, you're wearing a white dress and you look lovely.

(The clock strikes noon.)

And the clock struck that morning just the same way. *(Pause)* I remember when they carried father's coffin out there was a band playing, it was a military

3

funeral, and at the cemetery they fired rifles over the grave. He was a general, a brigade commander. I thought there should have been more people, but it was raining, raining hard, and then it started to snow.

IRINA: I don't want to think about it.

(Baron Túzenbach, Chebutýkin and Solyóny appear in the dining room.)

OLGA: Today it's warm enough to leave the windows wide open, even though the birch trees haven't put out any leaves yet. Father got his command eleven years ago and we left Moscow and came here, it was the beginning of May then too, I remember exactly, Moscow was already full of flowers, it was warm and there was sunshine everywhere. That was eleven years ago, and I remember it all exactly, just as if we'd only left Moscow yesterday. Oh, my! This morning I woke up and realized it was springtime, everything was so bright, I felt such a wave of happiness inside me, and I wanted so much to go back home.

CHEBUTYKIN: The hell you say!

TUZENBACH: You're right, it's all a lot of nonsense.

(Másha looks up absently and whistles under her breath.)

OLGA: Másha, don't whistle like that! Really! *(Pause)* I spend the whole day at school and then I do extra tutoring in the evenings, and my head aches all the time and I get so depressed sometimes, it's as if I'd gotten old all of a sudden. Four years at that high school, and every day I feel as if a little more life and strength was slipping away from me. There's only one thing that keeps me going . . .

IRINA: Moscow! Going back to Moscow! Selling this
house and everything and going back to Moscow . . .
OLGA: Yes. Going back to Moscow as soon as we can.

(Chebutýkin and Túzenbach laugh.)

IRINA: Brother of course will be a scientist, he certainly
can't go on living here. Only there *is* a problem about
poor Másha . . .
OLGA: Másha can come spend the summers with us, every
year.

(Másha whistles under her breath.)

IRINA: Well, I hope everything will work out. *(Looks out
the window)* The weather is wonderful today. I don't
know why I feel so good! This morning I remembered
it was my birthday, and all of a sudden I felt
wonderful, I thought about when I was little, when
mama was alive—I kept thinking the most wonderful
things!
OLGA: You do look lovely today, you seem really beautiful.
And Másha is beautiful too. Andréi would be better
looking, but he's gotten awfully heavy, it doesn't look
good on him. And I've gotten old. I've lost far too
much weight, I'm sure it's all because of the girls at
the high school, they keep making me so angry. But
today is Sunday, I can stay home, my head doesn't
ache, and I feel much younger than I did yesterday.
Well, that's all right, it's God's will, but sometimes I
think if I'd gotten married and could stay home all
day long, that would be better somehow. *(Pause)* I
would have loved my husband.
TUZENBACH *(To Solyóny)*: Nothing you say makes any

sense! I can't take it any more. *(Comes into the living room)* I forgot to tell you. Our new commanding officer is coming to pay you a visit today. Colonel Vershínin. *(Sits down at the piano)*

OLGA: Really? We'd be delighted.

IRINA: Is he old?

TUZENBACH: No, not at all. Maybe forty, forty-five at the most. *(Starts to play quietly)* He seems very nice. Definitely not stupid. He just talks a lot.

IRINA: Is he interesting?

TUZENBACH: I suppose so. He has a wife, a mother-in-law, and two little girls. And it's his second marriage. Everywhere he goes he tells people he has a wife and two little girls. Wait and see, he'll tell you too. His wife is a little crazy. She wears her hair in braids like a schoolgirl, she uses very highfalutin language, talks philosophy, and spends a lot of time trying to kill herself—mostly in order to annoy her husband, so far as I can tell. I would have left a woman like that long ago, but he just hangs on and complains about her.

(Solyóny comes into the living room with Chebutýkin.)

SOLYONY: I can only lift fifty pounds with one arm, but with two arms I can lift a hundred and fifty pounds, even more. What do I conclude from that? That two men are not just twice as strong as one, but three times as strong, or even more . . .

CHEBUTYKIN *(Reading his newspaper as he walks)*: To prevent falling hair. Two ounces of naphtha, in half a bottle of alcohol. Shake and use daily . . . *(Writes in a little notebook)* Well, let's just make a little note of that!

(To Solyóny) All right now, as I was saying, you take a cork, stick it in the bottle, then you get a little glass pipe and stick it through the cork. Then you take a pinch of ordinary, everyday baking soda . . .

IRINA: Iván Románich! Dear Iván Románich!

CHEBUTYKIN: What is it, child, what is it, dearest?

IRINA: Tell me why I feel so happy today! I feel as if I had sails flying in the wind, and the sky over me was bright blue and full of white birds. . . . Why is that? Do you know why?

CHEBUTYKIN *(Kissing both her hands tenderly)*: You're my little white bird . . .

IRINA: When I got up this morning everything in the world was suddenly clear, and I realized I knew how to live. Dear Iván Románich! I do know, everything. Man must work, work in the sweat of his brow. No matter who he is, that's the whole point of his life. And all his happiness. How wonderful it must be to get up at dawn and pave streets, or be a shepherd, or a school teacher who teaches children, or work on a railroad. My Lord, not even a man, a horse or something, as long as you work—anything's better than waking up at noon and having breakfast in bed and then taking two hours to dress. What an awful life that is! I want to work the way I want cold drinks in hot weather. And if I don't do that from now on, get up and go to work, then don't you ever have anything more to do with me, Iván Románich.

CHEBUTYKIN *(Tenderly)*: I won't, I promise . . .

OLGA: Father trained us all to get up at seven o'clock. Now Irína wakes up at seven and lies in bed for hours and thinks about things. And with such a serious face! *(Laughs)*

IRINA: You always treat me like a little girl! You think it's funny when I'm serious, but I'm twenty years old!

TUZENBACH: My God, I really understand that desire to work! I've never worked a day in my life. I was born in Petersburg, where it's cold and boring, and no one in my family has ever worked, or even had to worry. I remember whenever I got home from military school there was always a servant to take my boots off. I was a real little monster to them, but my mother just smiled and let me do whatever I wanted. She never understood when other people objected to the way I behaved. They tried to protect me from hardship, but I don't think they quite managed. And now the time has come, there's a storm gathering, a wild, elemental storm, it's coming, it's almost over our heads! And it will clean out our society, get rid of laziness and indifference, and this prejudice against working and this lousy rotten boredom. I intend to work, and in twenty-five or thirty years we will all work! All of us!

CHEBUTYKIN: Not me.

TUZENBACH: You don't count.

SOLYONY: In twenty-five years you won't be around, thank God. I give you a couple of years more; then you either die of a stroke, angel, or I shoot your head off. *(Takes out a little bottle of cologne and rubs some on his hands)*

CHEBUTYKIN *(Laughing)*: I never have done anything, ever. Once I graduated I never did another lick of work, I never read a single book. All I read are newspapers. *(Takes another newspaper out of his pocket)* For instance, I read in the papers, let's say, about a writer named Dobrolyúbov, so I know he exists, but God only knows what he wrote, I don't.

(Somebody knocks on the floor from below.)

Somebody wants me downstairs, I must have a visitor.
I'll be right back. . . . Just give me a minute or
so . . . *(Hurries out, combing his beard)*

IRINA: I think he's dreamed up another surprise.

TUZENBACH: You're right. Did you see the look on his
face as he went out? You are about to receive a
birthday present.

IRINA: That's so embarrassing.

OLGA: It really is terrible. He's always overdoing things.

MASHA. "Beside the sea there stands a tree, and on that
tree a golden chain . . . and on that tree a golden
chain . . ." *(Stands and hums quietly)*

OLGA: You're not very cheerful today, Másha.

(Másha keeps humming and puts on her hat.)

Where are you going?

MASHA: Home.

IRINA: That's rude.

TUZENBACH: . . . Leaving a birthday party!

MASHA: It's all right, I'll be back later on. Goodbye,
darling. *(Kisses Irína)* I want you to be well and
happy. When father was alive we used to have thirty
or forty officers at our birthday parties, it was noisy
and fun, and today there's only a man and a half and
it's dull as a desert. I'm leaving. I'm in a kind of
depressed mood today. I don't feel well, don't mind
what I say. *(Laughs, almost in tears)* We'll have a talk
later on, but goodbye for now, dear. I'm going for a
walk.

IRINA *(Upset)*: But what's the matter . . .

OLGA *(Tearfully)*: I know what you mean, Másha.

SOLYONY: When a man talks philosophy you get philosophy, or at least sophistry, but when a woman talks philosophy, or two women, all you get is wee, wee, wee, wee, all the way home.

MASHA: And exactly what is that supposed to mean?

SOLYONY: Nothing. "Said the dog to the flea, don't jump on me."

MASHA *(To Ólga, angrily)*: Oh, stop crying!

(Enter Anfísa, and Ferapónt with a birthday cake.)

ANFISA: Come on in. Come on, come on, it's all right, your feet are clean. *(To Irína)* It's a birthday cake. A present from Protopópov over at the council office.

IRINA: Thank you. *(Takes the cake)* Tell him thank you.

FERAPONT: What?

IRINA *(Louder)*: Tell him thank you.

OLGA: Nana, give him something to eat. Ferapónt, go on, she'll give you something to eat.

FERAPONT: What?

ANFISA: Come on, old man, come on, come on.

(She goes out with Ferapónt.)

MASHA: I don't like that Protopópov, or whatever his name is. You shouldn't have invited him.

IRINA: I didn't.

MASHA: Good.

(Chebutýkin comes in; he is followed by an orderly carrying a huge silver tea service. There is a general reaction of surprise and embarrassment.)

OLGA *(Making a gesture of exasperation)*: A silver service! How awful! *(Goes into the dining room)*

IRINA: Iván Románich, how could you?

TUZENBACH *(Laughing)*: What did I tell you!

MASHA: Iván Románich, you really are disgraceful!

CHEBUTYKIN: My dears, my little girls, you are all I have, you are dearer to me than anything else in the world. I'm sixty years old, I'm an old man, a lonely broken-down old man. The only decent thing left in me is my love for you; if it weren't for you I wouldn't have gone on living. *(To Irina)* Darling, I . . . my sweet little girl, I've known you since the day you were born . . . I carried you when you were a baby . . . I was in love with your sainted mother . . .

IRINA: But why such expensive presents?

CHEBUTYKIN *(Almost in tears; angrily)*: Expensive presents! Well, that's just . . . *(To the orderly)* Take it away. *(Mimicking her)* Expensive presents!

(Anfisa enters from the hall.)

ANFISA: There's a colonel just arrived, dears. Never laid eyes on him before. He's already got his coat off and everything. Rinie dear, you be nice to him. Mind your manners now. *(Leaving)* And it's long past lunchtime already. . . . Oh Lord . . .

TUZENBACH: It's probably Vershínin.

(Enter Vershínin.)

Lieutenant Colonel Vershínin!

VERSHININ *(To Másha and Irína)*: How do you do? I'm delighted to be here at last, delighted, believe me. Well, well! How you've grown!

IRINA: Won't you sit down. . . . It's very nice of you to come.

VERSHININ *(Happily)*: I'm delighted, really delighted! But there's three of you, isn't there? I remember three sisters, three little girls . . . I don't recall your faces, but I remember perfectly: your father, Colonel Prózorov, had three little girls. I saw you with my own eyes. Well, well, how time does fly!

TUZENBACH: Alexánder Ignátych is from Moscow.

IRINA: Moscow! You're from Moscow?

VERSHININ: Yes indeed. Your father was a battery commander in Moscow, and I was an officer in his command. *(To Másha)* Now your face I think I remember . . .

MASHA: Funny, I don't remember yours.

IRINA: Ólga! Ólga! *(Shouting into the dining room)* Ólga, come here!

(Ólga comes into the living room.)

Colonel Vershínin is from Moscow.

VERSHININ: You must be Ólga Sergéyevna, the oldest. And you are María. . . . And you are Irína, the youngest . . .

OLGA: You're from Moscow?

VERSHININ: Yes. I went to school in Moscow and began my service career there—served there quite a while, in fact, and I've finally gotten my own command—here, as you see. I don't remember you individually, all I remember is that there were three of you. Three sisters. I remember your father very well, when I close my eyes I can see him as if it were yesterday. I used to spend a lot of time at your house in Moscow . . .

OLGA: I thought I remembered everybody, but . . .

VERSHININ: Perhaps you remember my full name—
Alexánder Ignátych . . .

IRINA: Alexánder Ignátych, you're from
Moscow. . . . What a surprise!

OLGA: We're moving back there, you know.

IRINA: We expect to be there by autumn. It's our
hometown, we were born there. . . . On Old Basmány
Street . . .

(They both laugh delightedly.)

MASHA: We never expected to see anyone from Moscow
here. *(Excited)* Now I remember! Ólga, remember, they
used to tell us about "the love-sick major?" You were
a lieutenant then, and you were in love with someone,
and they used to tease you about being a major . . .

VERSHININ *(Laughing)*: Yes, yes, that's right. The love-sick
major, yes . . .

MASHA: You didn't have a moustache then. . . . Oh, you've
gotten old . . . *(Almost in tears)* You've gotten so old!

VERSHININ: Yes, when they called me the love-sick major
I was young and I was in love. Now I'm not.

OLGA: But you really don't look so bad. I mean, you've
gotten old, but you're not really . . . *old.*

VERSHININ: Well, I'm almost forty-four. How long has it
been since you left Moscow?

IRINA: Eleven years. Másha, what's the matter, don't cry,
you're so silly. *(Almost in tears)* You'll make me start.

MASHA: I'm all right. What street did you live on?

VERSHININ: On Old Basmány Street.

OLGA: So did we . . .

VERSHININ: Then for a while I lived on Nemétsky Street.

I used to walk from there to the barracks. You have to
cross a big bridge to get there, the water makes a
noise underneath you. If you're lonely it makes you
feel awful. *(Pause)* But the river you've got here is
wonderful! Wide, strong . . .

OLGA: Yes, but it gets cold here. It's cold, and there are
mosquitos . . .

VERSHININ: Oh come now, this is a very good climate,
very healthy, very Russian. The woods, the
river. . . . And you've got birch trees. Wonderful,
uncomplicated birch trees. They're my favorite tree.
Life here must be very good. But it's funny, the
nearest railroad station is eighteen miles away. And
nobody seems to know why.

SOLYONY: Well, I know why.

(Everybody looks at him.)

Because if the station were close it wouldn't be far
away, and if it's far away then it can't be close.

(An awkward silence.)

TUZENBACH: Very funny, Vassíly Vassílich.

OLGA: Oh, now I remember you. I really do.

VERSHININ: I knew your mother.

CHEBUTYKIN: She was a wonderful woman, God rest her.

IRINA: Mama is buried in Moscow.

OLGA: In Nóvo-Dévichy cemetery.

MASHA: It's funny, I'm beginning to forget what she
looked like. The same thing will happen to us. No
one will remember us.

VERSHININ: True. No one will remember us. That's fate,

there's nothing you can do about it. Things that seem important to us, serious and significant things—the time will come when they'll all be forgotten—or they won't seem so important anymore. *(Pause)* And the interesting thing is, there's no way we can guess what will be considered important and serious, and what will be considered petty and silly. Remember the discoveries of Copernicus, or let's say, Columbus, how they seemed silly and unnecessary at first, while a lot of nonsense was propounded as eternal truth? So in time perhaps this life of ours, the one we're so proud of, will seem strange, stupid, messy, perhaps even sinful . . .

TUZENBACH: But who knows? They may also think of the life we lead as a high point and remember it with respect. Today we have no torture, no capital punishment, no invasions, but there's still so much suffering . . .

SOLYONY: Wee, wee, wee . . . The Baron doesn't live on food like the rest of us, he just lives on philosophy!

TUZENBACH: Vassíly Vassílich, will you leave me alone, for godssakes? *(Changes his seat)* It's not funny anymore.

SOLYONY *(In a high voice)*: Wee, wee, wee, wee, wee . . .

TUZENBACH *(To Vershínin)*: . . . and the suffering observable everywhere today would seem to indicate that society has already attained a certain moral elevation . . .

VERSHININ: Yes, yes, of course.

CHEBUTYKIN: You just said, Baron, that people in the future will think of our life as a high point, but people nowadays are still pretty low. *(Stands up)* Look how low I am. But of course you make me feel better by calling my life a high point.

(A violin is played offstage.)

MASHA: That's our brother Andréi playing.

IRINA: He's the family intellectual. He'll probably be a
scientist. Papa was in the service, but his son has
decided on a scientific career.

MASHA: That's what Papa wanted him to do.

OLGA: We were teasing him today. He seems to be a little
bit in love.

IRINA: With one of the local girls. I imagine she'll be here
for lunch.

MASHA: But her clothes! It's not just that they're ugly, or
out of style, they're absolutely pitiful. She'll wear a
funny yellow skirt with some awful fringe, and a red
blouse. And those little pink cheeks, always scrubbed
clean, clean, clean! Andréi can't be in love, I don't
believe it. He does have *some* taste, after all. He's just
teasing us, that's all, he's acting silly. I heard someone
saying yesterday she's supposed to marry Protopópov,
the chairman of the county council, and I certainly
hope she does. *(Goes to the side door)* Andréi, come
here a minute! Just for a minute, dear.

(Andréi enters.)

OLGA: This is my brother, Andréi Sergéyich.

VERSHININ: Vershínin.

ANDREI: How do you do? *(Wipes his perspiring face)* You're
the new battery commander?

OLGA: Can you believe it, Colonel Vershínin is from
Moscow.

ANDREI: Are you? Well, congratulations, now my sisters
won't let you alone.

VERSHININ: I think I've already managed to bore your sisters.

IRINA: Look at this picture frame Andréi gave me for a present. *(Shows him the frame)* He made it himself.

VERSIIININ *(Looking at the frame and not knowing what to say)*: Yes, well, it certainly is . . .

IRINA: And this other frame over on the piano, he made that too.

(Andréi makes a deprecating gesture and starts off.)

OLGA: Andréi's our intellectual and he plays the violin and he can carve almost anything in wood, he's our genius. Andréi, don't go! He's always doing that, he wants to be alone. Come on back!

(Másha and Irina take his arms and lead him back, laughing.)

MASIIA. Cuine on, come on!

ANDREI: Please, don't . . .

MASHA: He's so funny! We all used to call Alexánder Ignátych the love-sick major, and he never got mad.

VERSHININ: Never!

MASHA: I've got a name for you: the love-sick violinist!

IRINA: Or the love-sick scientist!

OLGA: He's in love! Andréi's in love!

IRINA *(Applauding)*: Bravo, bravo! Encore! Andréi's in love!

CHEBUTYKIN *(Going up behind Andréi and grabbing him around the waist)*: "It's love that makes the world go round . . . !" *(Laughs; still has his newspaper)*

ANDREI: Will you all please stop it. *(Wipes his face)* I couldn't sleep all night and I feel sort of funny today—a little upset, I guess. I sat up reading until four and then I got into bed, but I just lay there. I

kept thinking about things, and all of a sudden the
sun came up and the bedroom was full of
light. . . . As long as I'm going to be here through the
summer, I want to translate this book from the
English . . .

VERSHININ: You read English?

ANDREI: Yes. My father, God rest him, educated us with a
vengeance. It's funny—and I guess it's sort of silly,
too, but you know, after he died I started putting on
weight, and in just a year I've gotten kind of heavy.
It's almost as if my body were letting itself go after all
that education. My father made sure that my sisters
and I knew French, German, and English and Irína
even knows Italian. But a lot of good it does us!

MASHA: What's the point of knowing three languages in a
town like this? It's a useless luxury. No, not even a
luxury; it's an unnecessary appendage, like a sixth
finger. We know a lot that's unnecessary.

VERSHININ: Well! *(Laughs)* You know a lot that's
unnecessary! I don't think there exists—I don't think
there *could* exist—a town so dull and boring that it
didn't have a real need for intelligent, educated
people. All right, let's agree that this town is
backward and vulgar, and let's suppose now that out
of all its thousands of inhabitants there are only three
people like you. Of course you won't be able to
overcome the unenlightened mass that surrounds you,
little by little you'll disappear into this crowd of
thousands, life will swallow you up. But you won't
simply disappear, you will have some influence. And
after you've gone there will be six more, let's say, like
you, then twelve, and so on, until finally people like
you will be in the majority. In two or three hundred

years life on earth will be unimaginably beautiful, astonishing. Man needs a life like that, and if we don't have it yet we must wait for it, dream of it, prepare for it, and that's the reason we must be able to see and know more than our fathers and grandfathers. *(Laughs)* And you complain that you know a lot that's unnecessary!

MASHA *(Taking off her hat)*: I'm staying for lunch.

IRINA *(Sighing)*: You know, you really ought to write all that down . . .

(Andréi has left unnoticed by now.)

TUZENBACH: You say life on earth will eventually be beautiful and wonderful. That's true. But in order for us to have a share in all that, even at this point, we have to get ready for it, we have to work . . .

VERSHININ: Yes. *(Gets up.)* What a lot of flowers you've got! *(Looks around)* And a beautiful house. I envy you. All my life I've lived in dumpy apartments with two chairs and a sofa, and the stove always smokes. And the one thing I've always wanted was a lot of flowers like this . . . *(Rubs his hands)* Oh, my! Well . . .

TUZENBACH: Yes, we have to *work*. Oh, I know you're all thinking, listen to the German getting sentimental again, but I'm really Russian, honestly I am, I don't even speak German. And my father was baptized in the Russian church.

(Pause.)

VERSHININ *(Walking around)*: Sometimes I think what it would be like to start life all over again, and do it deliberately. The life we'd already lived would be a kind of rough draft, and the new one would be a clean copy! And I think each of us would try not to repeat the same mistakes, at least try to arrange a new environment, find a room like this to live in, with flowers in it, and lots of light! I have a wife, and two little girls, and my wife is not a well woman, and what with one thing and another, if I could start life over again, believe me, I certainly wouldn't get married.

(Enter Kulýgin.)

KULYGIN *(Going up to Irína)*: Dearest sister, allow me to congratulate you on this happy occasion, and to convey to you my heartfelt wishes for good health and whatever else a girl of your age may desire—properly desire, that is. And allow me to present you with this little book as a small token of my esteem. *(Gives her a book)* It's a history of the first fifty years of our local high school. I wrote it myself. A mere trifle, written in an idle hour, but I want you to be sure to read it anyway. Ladies and gentlemen, good afternoon! *(To Vershínin)* Kulýgin. I teach at the local high school. *(To Irína)* This little book contains the names of all those who have graduated from our high school over the last fifty years. *Feci quod potui, faciant meliora potentes.* *(Kisses Másha)*

IRINA: But you gave me the same book as a present last Easter.

KULYGIN *(Laughing)*: No! Well, then give it back. Or better yet, give it to the Colonel. Here, Colonel. Read it some time when you have nothing better to do.

VERSHININ: Thank you. *(Gets ready to go)* I'm really
    delighted we've gotten to know each other again . . .
OLGA: Are you leaving? Oh, don't!
IRINA: You must stay and have lunch. Please.
OLGA: Do, really; please!
VERSHININ *(Bowing)*: I seem to have intruded on a
    birthday party. Excuse me, I didn't know, I should
    have congratulated you . . .

(He goes into the dining room with Ólga.)

KULYGIN: Today is Sunday, ladies and gentlemen, a day
    of rest. Let us all seek rest, each according to his age
    and status. These rugs should be rolled up and stored
    for the summer, in mothballs or naphtha. . . . The
    Romans were a healthy race, they knew how to work,
    they also knew how to rest. They had a *mens sana in
    corpore sano*. They lived their lives according to the
    proper forms. Our headmaster always says: the main
    thing in life is form. When things lose their form,
    they lose their identity—and in our daily lives it is
    precisely the same. *(Puts his arm around Másha's waist
    and laughs)* Másha loves me. My wife loves me. And
    the window drapes should be stored with the
    rugs. . . . I'm very happy today, in an excellent frame
    of mind. Másha, we're going to the headmaster's this
    afternoon at four. There's an outing for the teachers
    and their families.
MASHA: I'm not going.
KULYGIN *(Hurt)*: Másha dearest, why not?
MASHA: I'll tell you later . . . *(Angrily)* All right, all right,
    I'll go, only please just leave me alone . . . *(Moves
    away from him)*

KULYGIN: And he's invited us all back to spend the evening at his place. Despite his precarious health, that man does his best to be sociable. Astonishing personality. A remarkable man, really extraordinary. Yesterday at the faculty meeting he turned to me and said "I'm tired, Fyódor Ilých. Tired." *(Looks at the clock, then at his own watch)* Your clock is seven minutes fast. Tired. That's what he said.

(A violin is heard offstage.)

OLGA: Ladies and gentlemen, lunch is served! And the birthday cake!

KULYGIN: Ólga dearest! Ólga dearest! Yesterday I worked from early morning until eleven at night, I was tired. And today I feel very happy. *(Goes to the dinner table)* Dearest . . .

CHEBUTYKIN *(Folding his newspaper, putting it into his pocket and combing his beard)*: Birthday cake? Wonderful!

MASHA *(To Chebutýkin, severely)*: Now you listen to me: I don't want to see you drinking today! Understand? It's very bad for you.

CHEBUTYKIN: Oh, whoa, whoa, whoa, whoa. Now wait just a minute. I gave it up. I haven't been drunk in two years, for godssakes. Anyway, what difference does it make?

MASHA: Never mind, just don't drink, that's all. *(Angrily, but so that her husband can't hear her)* Another goddam boring evening at the headmaster's!

TUZENBACH: If I were you I just wouldn't go. It's very simple. Why not?

CHEBUTYKIN: Don't go, sweetheart . . .

MASHA: Oh fine, don't go, as easy as that. . . . What a miserable goddam life! *(Goes into the dining room)*

CHEBUTYKIN *(Going with her)*: Now, now . . .

SOLYONY *(Crossing to the dining room)*: Wee, wee, wee, wee . . .

TUZENBACH: That'll do, Vassíly Vassílich! Let it alone.

SOLYONY: Wee, wee, wee, wee, wee . . .

KULYGIN *(Happily)*: Your health, Colonel! I am a pedagogue by profession, but here I'm just one of the family, Másha's husband. She's a wonderful woman, a wonderful woman . . .

VERSHININ: I'll have a little of this dark vodka . . . *(Drinks)* Your health! *(To Ólga)* I feel very much at home here . . .

(Only Irína and Túzenbach are left in the living room.)

IRINA: Másha really feels awful today. She was only eighteen when she married him, and she thought he was very intelligent. Not anymore. He's a nice man, but he's not very intelligent.

OLGA *(Impatiently)*: Andréi, come on! We're all waiting for you!

ANDREI: I'm coming. *(Enters and crosses to the table)*

TUZENBACH: What are you thinking about?

IRINA: Oh, nothing. I don't like that Solyóny. I'm afraid of him. He says the stupidest things . . .

TUZENBACH: He's strange. I feel sorry for him. He makes me mad sometimes, but mostly I just feel sorry for him. I think he's really very shy. When there's just the two of us he's good company and quite intelligent, but whenever he's in a group he gets crude and vulgar, he always tries to start a fight. Don't go yet, let them all get settled first. Let me spend some time with you, just the two of us. What are you thinking about? *(Pause)* You're twenty years old, I'm not thirty yet. Think how much time we've got ahead of us, days and days, all of them full of my love for you . . .

IRINA: Nikolái Lvóvich, don't talk to me about love . . .

TUZENBACH *(Not listening)*: I have such a desire to live, Irína, and to work and fight for something, and my love for you makes that desire even stronger. You're so beautiful, you make life seem just as beautiful! What are you thinking about?

IRINA: You say life is so beautiful. But suppose it isn't? Look at us. Three sisters. Our life hasn't been so beautiful, it's choking us up like a lawn full of weeds. There, now I'm starting to cry. I really don't mean to . . . *(Wipes her eyes and smiles)* We have to work, we really do. The reason we're unhappy and think life is so awful is because we don't know what it means to work. We come from families who thought they never had to work . . .

(Enter Natásha; she wears a pink dress with a green belt.)

NATASHA: They're already eating . . . I guess I'm late . . . *(Stops briefly in front of the mirror and fixes herself up)* Well, at least my hair's okay. *(Seeing Irína)* Irína Sergéyevna, happy birthday! Congratulations, honey! *(Gives her a hug and several effusive kisses)* You've got so many guests, I feel sort of embarrassed. . . . Hello, Baron, how are *you*?

OLGA *(Coming into the living room)*: Well, if it isn't Natálya Ivánovna. How *are* you, my sweet?

(They exchange kisses.)

NATASHA: You've got such a big party I really feel awfully embarrassed . . .

OLGA: Now, now, none of that, it's all just friends . . . *(Lowers her voice, a bit shocked)* A green belt! Darling, that just isn't done!

NATASHA: Why, is it bad luck or something?

OLGA: No, it just doesn't look right with that dress . . . well, it looks a bit odd, that's all.

NATASHA *(In a whiny voice)*: But why? It isn't really *so* green, I mean, it's more, you know, green-*ish* . . .

(She follows Ólga into the dining room. Everyone is now at the table; the living room is empty.)

KULYGIN: Irína dearest, here's hoping you find a suitable fiance. It's about time you got married.

CHEBUTYKIN: Here's hoping Natálya Ivánovna finds herself a boyfriend too.

KULYGIN: Natálya Ivánovna already has a boyfriend.

MASHA *(Banging her plate with a fork)*: I'll have another little glass of that wine. Well, we only live once, by God, and sometimes you win, sometimes you lose.

KULYGIN: You get an F-minus in conduct.

VERSHININ: This vodka is delicious. What gives it that special taste?

SOLYONY: Cockroach juice.

IRINA *(Crybaby voice)*: *Oh!* That's dis*gus*ting!

OLGA: We're having roast turkey and apple pie for dinner tonight. Thank God, I've got the whole day off, and the evening too . . . I hope you'll all be able to come for dinner.

VERSHININ: I hope you'll let me come, too.

IRINA: Of course.

NATASHA: They're very informal around here.

CHEBUTYKIN: "It's love that makes the world go
round . . ." *(Laughs)*

ANDREI *(Angry)*: Will you all please stop it! Aren't you
tired of it yet?

(Fedótik and Róhde enter with a big basket of flowers.)

FEDOTIK: Oh, they're already having lunch.

ROHDE *(In a deep, loud voice, with exaggerated r's)*: Lunch?
Yes, it's true, they are already having lunch!

FEDOTIK: Wait a minute! *(Takes a picture)* There! Now
one more . . . everybody hold still! *(Takes another
picture)* There! Now you can all move!

*(They take the basket of flowers and go into the dining room,
where everyone greets them noisily.)*

ROHDE *(In a loud voice)*: Happy birthday and best wishes!
The very best! The weather is just wonderful today,
really beautiful. I took some of the high school boys
out for a walk this morning. I'm the gymnastics coach
at the high school . . .

FEDOTIK: That's all right, Irína Sergéyevna, you don't
have to hold still, it's all right! *(Takes a picture)* You
look very interesting today. *(Takes a top out of his
pocket)* Oh, I forgot. A present for you, a top. It
makes an amazing sound . . .

IRINA: Oh, it's divine!

MASHA: "Beside the sea there stands a tree, and on that
tree a golden chain . . . and on that chain an educated
cat goes around and around and around . . ."

(Tearfully) Why do I keep saying that? I can't get it out of my head . . .

KULYGIN: There are thirteen of us at the table!

ROHDE *(In a loud voice)*: Surely, ladies and gentlemen, you are above such silly superstitions?

(Laughter.)

KULYGIN: If there are thirteen at table, that means two of them are in love. Iván Románich, I certainly hope nobody's in love with *you* . . .

(Laughter.)

CHEBUTYKIN: Oh, not me, I'm just an old boozer. But look at Natálya Ivánovna, what do you suppose she's got to blush about?

(Everybody laughs loudly; Natásha gets up and runs into the living room. Andréi follows her.)

ANDREI: It's all right, don't pay any attention to them! Wait. . . . Don't go, please . . .

NATASHA: I'm so embarrassed. I just don't know what's the matter with me, they just make fun of me all the time. I know it's not polite to leave the table like that, but I just couldn't stand it, I really couldn't . . . *(Hides her face in her hands)*

ANDREI: Oh, darling, please, please don't get upset. They're only joking, honestly they are, they all mean well. Darling, they're all nice people, they love me and they love you too. Come on over here by the window, they can't see us over here . . . *(Looks around)*

NATASHA: It's just that I'm not used to these social
   occasions . . .

ANDREI: Oh, you're so young, so young and beautiful!
   Darling, oh, darling, don't get upset. Believe me,
   believe me . . . I feel so good, I feel so full of love
   and I'm so proud. . . . Oh, they can't see us! Don't
   worry, they can't see us. I don't know how I fell in
   love with you, or when, or why—I just don't
   understand any of it. Darling, you're so sweet and so
   ordinary . . . I want you to marry me! I love you, I
   love you . . . I've never loved anybody before . . .

*(They kiss. Two officers enter, see them kissing, and stop in
amazement.)*

CURTAIN

Act Two

The same set as Act One. Eight o'clock at night. Somewhere at a distance, someone in the street is playing an accordion. The room is dark.

Enter Natásha in a housecoat, carrying a candle. She crosses to the door to Andréi's room and stops.

NATASHA: Andy, what you doing? You reading? It's okay, I just wanted to . . . (Goes to another door, opens it, looks in, closes it) The lamps aren't lit . . .

ANDREI (Coming in with a book in his hand): What's the matter, Natásha?

NATASHA: I was just looking to see if the lamps were lit. Tonight's carnival, the maid's all in a tizzy, you got to keep your eyes on them so nothing happens. Last night after midnight I was going through the dining room and there was this candle burning. I never could find out who did it. (Puts down the candle) What time is it?

ANDREI (Looking at the clock): Quarter after eight.

NATASHA: And Ólga and Irína are still out. Haven't come
home yet. They just work and work, poor dears. Ólga
at the Board of Education, Irína at the telegraph
office . . . *(Sighs)* This morning I told your sister, I
said you take care of yourself Irína, you hear me,
honey? She never listens. Did you say quarter after
eight? I'm worried about Bobik, I think maybe he's a
little sick. Why is he so cold? Yesterday he had a
fever, and today he's cold all over . . . I get so
worried!

ANDREI: He's all right, Natásha. The baby's all right.

NATASHA: Well, all the same I better start him on a
different diet. I'm just worried. And they said the
carnival people are supposed to come tonight, I just
don't think they better, Andy.

ANDREI: Look, I don't know. They *were* invited.

NATASHA: This morning the baby woke up and looked at
me, and all of a sudden he smiled and I just know he
recognized me. Hello, Bobik, I said, hello, darlin'.
And he laughed. Babies know exactly what's going on,
Andy, they really do. So . . . I guess I'll just tell them
not to let the carnival people in when they come.

ANDREI *(Hesitantly)*: Well, whatever my sisters say. It's
their house, it's up to them.

NATASHA: Them too, I'll tell them too. They're so sweet.
(Gets up to go) I told them to get you some yoghurt
for supper. Doctor says you shouldn't eat anything
except yoghurt otherwise you're not ever going to lose
weight. *(Stops)* Bobik's cold. I'm worried he's going to
catch cold in that room of his, he could, you know?
We should move him into another room until the
warm weather comes. For instance Irína's room is just
right for a baby's room, it's dry and gets the sun all

day long. We should tell her, and she can move in
with Ólga until then. . . . She's never here during the
daytime anyway, she just spends the night here . . .
(Pause) Andy, how come you never talk to me?

ANDREI: Nothing, I was just thinking. . . . What is there
to say?

NATASHA: Yeah. . . . There was something else I wanted
to tell you. . . . Oh yes. Ferapónt from the council is
here, he says he has to talk to you . . .

ANDREI *(Yawning)*: Tell him to come in.

*(Natásha goes out. Andréi sits by the candle she has left and
reads his book. Ferapónt comes in. He is wearing an old tattered
overcoat with the collar turned up and his scarf tied over his
ears.)*

Hello, old man. What's up?

FERAPONT: Chairman sent over a book and some papers.
Here. *(Gives him a book and a packet)*

ANDREI: Thanks. That's fine. Why did you come by so
late? It's already after eight.

FERAPONT: What?

ANDREI *(Louder)*: I said, you came by late. It's already
after eight.

FERAPONT: That's right. I came by a while ago, it was
still light. Wouldn't let me in. Said you were busy.
That's what they said. Well, that's fine, if he's busy
he's busy. I'm not in no hurry. *(Thinks Andréi asked
him something)* What?

ANDREI: Nothing. *(Looks through the book)* Tomorrow's
Friday, there's no meeting, but I'll go in anyway . . .
get something done. It's a bore around here . . .
(Pause) How funny life is! Today I had nothing to do,

I was bored, I picked up this book—my old lecture
notes from the University, and I started to
laugh. . . . My God, I'm the secretary of the county
council, the same council that Protopópov is chairman
of, I'm the secretary, and the highest honor I can
hope for is to become a full member! Me, a member
of the local county council, and every night I dream
I'm a professor at the University of Moscow, a famous
scientist, the pride of Russia!

FERAPONT: I dunno. . . . Can't hear too well.

ANDREI: If you could hear I wouldn't be telling you all of
this. I have to talk to someone, my wife doesn't
understand me, I'm afraid of my sisters, I don't know
why . . . I'm always afraid they'll laugh at me, make
me feel ashamed. . . . I don't drink, I don't like bars,
but I'd love to be in Moscow right now, sitting at a
table at Téstov's or the Grand Moscow.

FERAPONT: Now in Moscow, there's a fella over to the
office the other day, he says there was this bunch of
men in Moscow, businessmen, he says, and they were
eatin' pancakes. Now this one fella, he ate forty of
'em, he up and died. Or maybe it was fifty. Can't
remember.

ANDREI: In Moscow you can sit in a restaurant full of
people, and nobody knows you and you don't know
anybody, but still you don't feel like a stranger. In
this town you know everybody and everybody knows
you, but you're always a stranger. . . . A stranger, and
alone.

FERAPONT: What? *(Pause)* This same fella, he was tellin'
us—coulda been lyin', I dunno—he was sayin', they
got a rope in Moscow, hangs all across town, one side
to the other.

ANDREI: What's it for?

FERAPONT: I dunno. This fella was tellin' us.

ANDREI: He made it up. *(Reads the book)* Were you ever in Moscow?

FERAPONT: Nope. Things just didn't work out that way. *(Pause)* Mind if I go?

ANDREI: Sure. Take care of yourself.

(Ferapónt goes out.)

Take care of yourself. Come over tomorrow, will you, and pick up these papers—wait a minute . . . *(Pause)* He's gone.

(The doorbell rings.)

That's it, work . . .

(He stretches and goes slowly to his room. Offstage a nurse sings a lullaby to the baby. Enter Másha and Vershínin. While they talk, the maid lights the lamps and candles in the room.)

MASHA: I don't know. *(Pause)* I don't know. Of course, habit can be very strong. For example, after father died it took us a long time to get used to the fact that we didn't have orderlies anymore. But I think I'm being fair about it, even allowing for habit. Maybe it's different in other places, but in this town the most respectable, the best brought up and the best educated people are in the military.

VERSHININ: I'm really thirsty. I'd love a cup of tea.

MASHA *(Looking at the clock)*: It ought to be ready in a minute. I got married when I was eighteen, and I was afraid of my husband because he was a teacher, and I

was barely out of school. I used to think he was
terribly wise, intelligent, and important. Now I've
changed my mind. Unfortunately.

VERSHININ: Yes. Well . . .

MASHA: Oh, I don't mean my husband. I've gotten used
to him. But most of the people in this town are so
vulgar, so unpleasant, so stupid. Vulgarity upsets me,
it wounds me, I get physically sick when I see
someone who lacks finesse, who lacks kindness and
gentleness. When I have to spend time with my
husband's colleagues from the high school it makes me
sick.

VERSHININ: Well . . . I don't see that much difference,
though, between military and civilians—in this town
at least. They both seem uninteresting. They're all
alike! Listen to any one of the locals who claims to be
sensitive or intelligent—civilian or military. His wife
depresses him, his house depresses him, everything he
owns depresses him. We are all supposed to be such
highly developed abstract thinkers, but why are our
lives so depressing? Why?

MASHA: Why?

VERSHININ: Why does his wife depress him? And his
children? And why do they get depressed by him?

MASHA: You're a bit depressed yourself today.

VERSHININ: Maybe. I didn't have lunch today. I haven't
eaten a thing since this morning. My daughter wasn't
feeling well, and whenever something is the matter
with my two little girls I always get very upset, it
kills me to think of the mother they've got. God, you
should have seen her this morning! What a fool she is!
We started fighting at seven this morning, and at nine

I slammed the door and left. *(Pause)* I never talk about these things. It's funny, you're the only one I complain to about it . . . *(Kisses her hand)* Don't be angry with me. You're absolutely all I've got.

(Pause.)

MASHA: Listen to the noise in the chimney. Right before father died the wind made a noise in the chimney. Just like that.

VERSHININ: Are you superstitious?

MASHA: Yes.

VERSHININ: That's strange. *(Kisses her hand)* You're a strange, wonderful woman. Strange and wonderful. I can see your eyes shining in the dark.

MASHA *(Moving to another chair)*: There's more light over here.

VERSHININ: I love you, I love you, I love your eyes, the way you move, I dream about you. . . . You strange, wonderful woman!

MASHA *(Laughing quietly)*: When you talk to me that way it makes me laugh somehow—even though it terrifies me. Don't say it again, please . . . *(Half to herself)* No, go on, say it, what difference does it make? *(Makes an exasperated gesture)* It doesn't make any difference. Someone's coming, talk about something else . . .

(Irína and Túzenbach enter through the dining room.)

TUZENBACH: I have a triple family name. Baron Túzenbach-Króne-Áltschauer, but I'm Russian just like you, I was baptized in the Russian church. There's very little German left in me, except for patience—stubbornness, I guess it seems to you. I walk you home every night.

IRINA: I'm so tired.

TUZENBACH: And every evening I'll show up at the telegraph office and walk you home, I promise, for the next ten or twenty years, until you chase me away . . . *(Notices Másha and Vershínin, delightedly)* Oh, it's you! Hello!

IRINA: Home at last. *(To Másha)* A lady came in tonight to send a telegram to her brother in Sarátov, her son died today, and she couldn't remember the address. So she sent it without one, just to Sarátov. She was crying. And I was rude to her, for no reason. "I'm in a hurry," I said. It was such a stupid thing to do. Are the carnival people coming tonight?

MASHA: Yes.

IRINA *(Sitting down in an armchair)*: I've got to get some rest. I'm worn out.

TUZENBACH *(With a smile)*: Whenever you get off work you look so little, so helpless . . .

(Pause.)

IRINA: I'm tired. I hate the telegraph office. I hate it.

MASHA: You've lost weight. *(Whistles softly)* It makes you look younger, your face is like a boy's.

TUZENBACH: That's because of the way she wears her hair.

IRINA: I've got to find another job, this one is all wrong for me. Whatever it was I wanted or was dreaming of—this is definitely not it. It's work, but there's no poetry in it, no meaning in it . . .

(A knock on the floor from below.)

The Doctor's knocking. *(To Túzenbach)* You knock, dear, will you? I haven't got the strength—I'm worn out . . .

(Túzenbach knocks on the floor.)

He'll be right up. Listen, we have got to do something. Last night the Doctor and Andréi were playing cards at the club and they lost again. Somebody said Andréi lost two hundred rubles.

MASHA *(Apathetic)*: What can we do about it now?

IRINA: Two weeks ago he lost, in December he lost. I wish he'd hurry up and lose everything, then maybe we could get out of town. Oh my God, I dream about Moscow night after night, sometimes I think I'm going absolutely crazy. *(Laughs)* We're moving in June, so that leaves . . . February, March, April, May . . . almost half a year!

MASHA: The main thing is not to let Natásha find out he's lost all that money.

IRINA: I don't think she even cares.

(Chebutýkin enters, combing his beard. He has just gotten up from a nap after dinner. He sits down at the dining room table and takes a newspaper out of his pocket.)

MASHA: Here he comes. Has he paid his rent?

IRINA *(Laughing)*: No. Not for the last eight months. I guess he forgot.

MASHA: Look at him sit there!

(Everybody laughs; pause.)

IRINA: Why are you so quiet, Alexánder Ignátych?

VERSHININ: I don't know. I want some tea! My kingdom

for a cup of tea! I haven't eaten a thing since this
morning . . .

CHEBUTYKIN: Irína Sergéyevna!

IRINA: What do you want?

CHEBUTYKIN: Please come here. *Venez ici.*

(Irína crosses and sits down at the table.)

I can't do without you.

(Irína lays out a game of solitaire.)

VERSHININ: Now what? If we're not going to have tea,
let's talk.

TUZENBACH: All right, let's do. What about?

VERSHININ: What about? Let's make up things. For
instance, let's talk about what life will be like after
we're gone, say in two hundred or three hundred
years.

TUZENBACH: Well, after we're gone people will travel
around in flying machines, they'll wear different style
jackets, maybe they'll discover a sixth sense and
expand our perceptions, but life won't change. It will
still be hard and happy and mysterious. Three
hundred years from now people will still go around
complaining, "Oh, life is so hard," and they will still
be afraid to die, the same as they are now.

VERSHININ *(Thinking a bit)*: No! How can I make myself
clear? I believe that everything in the world will
change, little by little; it's already changing right
before our eyes. In two or three hundred years, well
in a thousand, maybe—the number of years isn't so
important—a new and a happier life will begin. Of
course we'll never see it, but we are working towards

it right now. We work for it, we suffer for it, we create it, in fact. And that's the whole point of our existence. That's what happiness is, I think.

(Másha laughs softly.)

TUZENBACH: What are you laughing about?
MASHA: I don't know. I started laughing this morning and I've been laughing all day long.
VERSHININ: I graduated from the same school you did, even though I never went to the Academy; I read a lot, but I'm not very good at choosing books, sometimes I think I'm reading all the wrong things. Still, the longer I live the more I want to know. My hair is turning gray, I'm almost an old man, and I know so little—so little! But all the same I think I do know the most important thing. The only real thing. And I want to convince you of it, too. That happiness doesn't exist as yet, it will never exist for us, and that's all right, that's as it should be. . . . Our task is only to work and work; happiness is reserved for our descendants. *(Pause)* It's not for me. It's for my distant descendants.

(Fedótik and Róhde appear in the dining room; they sit down and hum softly, strumming a guitar.)

TUZENBACH: According to you, we can't even dream of happiness! But what if I'm happy already?
VERSHININ: You're not.
TUZENBACH *(Making a deprecating gesture and laughing)*: Obviously we are on opposite sides of the fence. Now how am I going to convince you?

(Másha laughs softly. He shakes a finger at her.)

Go ahead and laugh! *(To Vershínin)* Not just in two or three hundred years, but even in a million years life will still be the same as it's always been. It doesn't change, it always stays the same, it has its own laws which are none of your business, or at least you'll never find out what they are. Birds that migrate, cranes for instance, just fly and fly, and no matter what thoughts they may be thinking, great thoughts or small thoughts, they keep on flying without knowing where or why. They fly, and they will always fly, no matter what great philosophers may arise among them; they can talk philosophy if they want, but they can never stop flying . . .

MASHA: But there has to be some meaning in it . . .

TUZENBACH: Meaning? Look out the window: it's snowing. Is there any meaning in that?

(Pause.)

MASHA: I think a person has to believe in something, or has to look for something to believe in, otherwise his life is empty, empty. . . . Just to live, and not to know why the cranes fly, why children are born, why there are stars in the sky. . . . Either you know the reason why you're alive, or nothing makes any difference.

(Pause.)

VERSHININ: Still, it's too bad youth doesn't last . . .

MASHA: You know what Gogol said: Ladies and gentlemen, life is a bore!

TUZENBACH: And I say: Ladies and gentlemen, arguing is a bore! With you anyway . . .

CHEBUTYKIN *(Reading from the newspaper)*: Balzac was married in Berdíchev.

(Irína hums to herself.)

Let's just make a little note of that one. *(Writes)* Balzac was married in Berdíchev. *(Goes back to his paper)*

IRINA *(Laying out a game of solitaire, thoughtfully)*: Balzac was married in Berdíchev.

TUZENBACH: Well, the die is cast. María Sergéyevna, did you know I'm resigning from the military?

MASHA: So I heard. I don't know what's so wonderful about it. I hate civilians.

TUZENBACH: What difference does it make? *(Gets up)* I'm not very good-looking, what kind of military man is that? Anyway it doesn't make any difference, really it doesn't . . . I'm going to work. At least once in my life I'm going to work so hard I'll come home at night and fall into bed all worn out and go right to sleep. *(Goes into the dining room)* Working people must sleep very well.

FEDOTIK *(To Irína)*: I was down on Moscow street today and I bought these for you at Pyzhikov's. Crayons. And a little knife . . .

IRINA: You always treat me like a little girl, but I *am* grown up, you know . . . *(With delight, as she takes the crayons and the knife)* Oh, they're divine!

FEDOTIK: And I got a knife for myself too. . . . Look. Here's one blade, and another one, and another one,

and this is for cleaning your ears, and this is a pair of
scissors, and this is for cleaning your nails . . .

ROHDE *(Loud voice)*: Doctor, how old are you?

CHEBUTYKIN: Me? Thirty-two.

(Laughter.)

FEDOTIK: Here, do you want me to show you another way
to play solitaire?

*(He lays out the game. They bring in things for tea. Anfisa
busies herself with the tea; soon Natásha comes in and busies
herself at the table as well. Solyóny comes in, says hello to people
and sits down at the table.)*

VERSHININ: Listen to that wind!

MASHA: Yes, winter's a bore. I can't even remember what
summer is like.

IRINA: Look, the solitaire is coming out. That means we'll
get to Moscow.

FEDOTIK: No it isn't. See, you've got an eight on a two of
spades. *(Laughs)* That means you won't get to
Moscow.

CHEBUTYKIN *(Reading the newspaper)*: Tsítsikar. An
epidemic of smallpox has broken out here.

ANFISA *(To Másha)*: Másha dear, tea's ready.

MASHA: Bring mine here, Nana. I can't budge!

IRINA: Nana!

ANFISA: *Coming!*

NATASHA *(To Solyóny)*: Little babies understand
everything you say. "Hi, Bobik," I said, "Hello,
darlin'." And you should have *seen* the way he looked
at me. Oh, I know what you think, I'm just his

mother, but it's more than that, believe you me. He's an extraordinary child.

SOLYONY: If that child were mine, I would have sauteed him in butter and eaten him long ago. *(Takes his tea into the living room and sits in a far corner)*

NATASHA *(Making a gesture of exasperation)*: Oh, that man is so crude and vulgar!

MASHA: How wonderful it must be not to know whether it's winter or summer. I think if I lived in Moscow I wouldn't care what the weather was.

VERSHININ: The other day I was reading the diary of that French politician, the one who went to prison because of the Panama scandal. It was so moving the way he described the birds he could see from his prison window, birds he never even noticed when he was a government official. Of course now that he's out of prison he probably doesn't notice them anymore. It's the same with you: once you're actually living in Moscow you won't notice it anymore either. We're never happy, we can never be happy. We only *want* to be happy.

TUZENBACH *(Taking a box from the table)*: What happened to the candy?

IRINA: Solyóny ate it.

TUZENBACH: He ate it *all?*

ANFISA *(Handing Vershínin a cup of tea)*: Somebody brought a note for you, dear.

VERSHININ: For me? *(Takes it)* It's from my daughter. *(Reads it)* Oh God, wouldn't you know. . . . Excuse me, María Sergéyevna, I have to go. I'll just slip out quietly. I can't stay for tea. *(Stands up, upset)* It's the same old story . . .

MASHA: What's the matter? I hope it's not a secret.

VERSHININ *(Quietly)*: My wife has taken too many pills again. I have to go. I'll go out this way. It's all very unpleasant. *(Kisses Másha's hand)* My dearest, you wonderful woman . . . I'll just go out quietly . . . *(Leaves)*

ANFISA: Now where's he going? I just gave him his tea! Really, I never saw the likes . . .

MASHA *(Flaring up)*: Go away! You just stand there bothering me all the time . . . *(Goes with her teacup to the table)* I'm sick and tired of that old woman . . .

ANFISA: Now what's gotten into her? My lord!

ANDREI'S VOICE: Anfísa!

ANFISA *(Mimicking him)*: Anfísa! He just sits there . . . *(Goes out)*

MASHA *(At the dining room table, angrily)*: Give me some room to sit down! *(Shoves the cards to one side)* You've got cards all over the place. Drink your tea!

IRINA: Másha, you're being mean.

MASHA: Well if I am, don't talk to me! Just leave me alone.

CHEBUTYKIN *(Laughing)*: Leave her alone, leave her alone . . .

MASHA: And you! You're sixty years old and all you do is talk a lot of goddam nonsense, just like some kid!

NATASHA *(Sighing)*: Másha dear, why do you always use language like that! You have a very attractive personality, and I'm sure you could make a real nice impression on social occasions, I'll tell you quite frankly, if it weren't for those vulgar words of yours. *Je vous prie, pardonnez-moi, Marie, mais vous avez des manières un peu grossières.*

TUZENBACH *(Choking back a laugh)*: Give me . . . oh, give me . . . there . . . I think there's some cognac . . .

NATASHA: *Il parait que mon Bobik déjà ne dort pas*, he woke
up. He hasn't been feeling well all day. I'll just go
take a look, excuse me . . . *(Goes out)*

IRINA: Where did Alexánder Ignátych go?

MASHA: Home. There's something going on with his wife
again.

TUZENBACH *(Going up to Solyóny with the decanter of cognac
in his hands)*: You're always sitting off by yourself
thinking about something—only nobody ever knows
what. Listen, let's be friends. Have a drink.

(They drink.)

I've got to play the piano tonight, all night,
probably—just silly stuff. Well, that's all right.

SOLYONY: What do you mean, be friends? Who said we
were enemies?

TUZENBACH: You always make me feel as if something
had gone wrong between us. You're kind of strange,
you must admit . . .

SOLYONY *(Reciting)*: I am strange, we all are strange!
Forget thy wrath, Aléko!

TUZENBACH: Aléko? Who's Aléko?

(Pause.)

SOLYONY: Whenever I'm alone with someone, I feel all
right, just ordinary, but when I'm in a group I feel
depressed, and shy and I . . . I say a lot of stupid
things. But still, I'm more honest and open than a lot
of other people. A lot of others. And I can prove it.

TUZENBACH: I know I get mad at you a lot, you're always
trying to pick a fight with me whenever we're out

anywhere, but I still like you anyway. What the hell. I
feel like getting drunk tonight. Let's have a drink!

SOLYONY: Let's have a drink.

(They drink.)

I don't have anything against you, Baron. But I have
the soul of Lérmontov. *(Quietly)* I even look a little
like Lérmontov. . . . At least that's what people
say . . . *(Takes out his bottle of cologne and rubs some on
his hands)*

TUZENBACH: I'm resigning from the service. *Basta!* I've
been thinking about it for five years and I finally
decided to do it. I'm going to go to work.

SOLYONY *(Reciting)*: Forget thy wrath, Aléko! Forget thy
dreams . . .

*(While they talk, Andréi comes in with his book and sits near a
lamp.)*

TUZENBACH: I'm going to work.

CHEBUTYKIN *(Going into the living room with Irína)*: And
it was a real caucasian dinner too: we had onion soup,
and a meat dish called *chekhartmá.*

SOLYONY: *Cheremshá* isn't meat, it's a kind of onion.

CHEBUTYKIN: No, no, angel. *Chekhartmá* isn't an onion,
it's a meat dish, made with lamb.

SOLYONY: And I'm telling you *cheremshá* is an onion.

CHEBUTYKIN: And I'm telling you *chekhartmá* is a meat
dish.

SOLYONY: And I'm telling you *cheremshá* is an onion.

CHEBUTYKIN: What am I arguing with you for? You were
never in the Caucasus and you've never eaten
chekhartmá!

SOLYONY: I've never eaten *cheremshá* because I can't stand it. It tastes worse than garlic!

ANDREI *(Imploring)*: That's enough! Will you two please stop it?

TUZENBACH: When are the carnival people coming?

IRINA: They should be here now; they promised to come around nine.

TUZENBACH *(Hugging Andréi and singing)*: *Akh, vy seni, moyi seni, seni novye moyi . . .*

ANDREI *(Dancing and singing)*: *Seni novye, klenovye . . .*

CHEBUTYKIN *(Dancing)*: *Reshochatye!*

(Laughter.)

TUZENBACH: Goddam it, let's have a drink. Andy, let's drink to being friends. And I'll go with you, Andy, to the university in Moscow.

SOLYONY: Which one? There are two universities in Moscow.

ANDREI: There's only one university in Moscow.

SOLYONY: And I'm telling you there are two.

ANDREI: I don't care if there are three. The more the merrier.

SOLYONY: There are two universities in Moscow!

(Booing and hissing.)

There are two universities in Moscow: the old university and the new university. And if it bothers you all to listen to me, if my words offend you, I don't have to say anything. I can even leave the room . . . *(Goes out)*

TUZENBACH: Bravo, bravo! *(Laughs)* All right, ladies and gentlemen, here we go! I am about to play! That

Solyóny is a clown . . . *(Sits down at the piano, plays a waltz)*

MASHA *(Waltzing by herself)*: The Baron is drunk, the Baron is drunk, the Baron is drunk!

(Enter Natásha.)

NATASHA *(To Chebutýkin)*: Iván Románich!

(She whispers something to Chebutýkin, then goes out quietly. Chebutýkin taps Túzenbach on the shoulder and whispers something; he stops playing.)

IRINA: What's the matter?

CHEBUTYKIN: It's time for us to go. Goodnight now.

TUZENBACH: Goodnight. It's time to go.

IRINA: Excuse me—but what about the carnival people?

ANDREI *(Embarrassed)*: They're not coming. Well, you see, dear, Natásha says that Bobik isn't feeling well, and so. . . . Look, I don't know, what difference does it make?

IRINA *(Shrugging her shoulders)*: Bobik isn't feeling well!

MASHA: Well, sometimes you win, sometimes you lose. If they kick us out, then I guess we go. *(To Irína)* Bobik isn't sick, she is! In the head! *(Points a finger at her head)* That cheap little . . .

(Andréi goes into his own room, Chebutýkin follows him. In the dining room everyone is saying goodbye.)

FEDOTIK: What a shame! I was really counting on spending the evening, but if the baby is sick, of course. . . . I'll bring him a little present to-morrow . . .

ROHDE *(Loudly)*: Today I took a long nap after dinner on purpose, because I thought we'd be up all night dancing. It's not even ten o'clock yet!

MASHA: Let's go out in front of the house, we can talk there. Let's think of someplace else to go.

(We hear: "Goodbye!" "Goodnight!" Túzenbach's happy laugh. Everybody leaves. Anfisa and the maid clear the table and turn out the lamps. The nurse is singing somewhere. Andréi, in an overcoat and hat, and Chebutýkin enter quietly.)

CHEBUTYKIN: I never managed to get married because life just went by like a flash, and also because I was crazy in love with your mother and she was already married . . .

ANDREI: Nobody should get married. It's boring.

CHEBUTYKIN: Maybe so, but loneliness is worse. No matter how you rationalize it, my boy, loneliness is an awful business. Although when you get right down to it, actually—what difference does it make?

ANDREI: Come on, let's go.

CHEBUTYKIN: What are you in such a rush for? We'll make it.

ANDREI: I'm afraid my wife might stop me.

CHEBUTYKIN: Oh.

ANDREI: Tonight I'm not going to play cards, I'm just going to sit and watch. I don't feel very well. What are you supposed to do for pains in your chest, Iván Románich?

CHEBUTYKIN: Don't ask me. I don't know, my boy, I can't remember.

ANDREI: Let's go out the back way.

(They leave. The doorbell rings, then again. Voices and laughter.)

IRINA *(Entering)*: Who is that?
ANFISA *(In a whisper)*: The carnival people!

(The doorbell.)

IRINA: Tell them there's nobody home, Nana. And say we're sorry.

(Anfisa leaves. Irína wanders about the room thinking; she is upset. Enter Solyóny.)

SOLYONY *(Bewildered)*: There's no one here. . . . Where did everybody go?
IRINA: They went home.
SOLYONY: That's funny. Are you alone?
IRINA: Yes. *(Pause)* Goodnight.
SOLYONY: I behaved badly before; I lost control, it was tactless. But you're not like the others, you're different, you are pure and distant, you understand the truth. . . . You're the only one who can understand me, the only one. I love you . . . I love you deeply, endlessly . . .
IRINA: Goodnight! Please go.
SOLYONY: I can't live without you. *(Goes up to her)* You're divine! What happiness! You have wonderful eyes, brilliant, disturbing eyes. I've never seen a woman with eyes like yours before . . .
IRINA *(Coldly)*: Stop it, Vassíly Vassílich!
SOLYONY: This is the first time I've ever talked about my love for you. *(Rubs his forehead)* Well, maybe it doesn't make any difference. I can't force you to be nice to

me, I know that. . . . But no happy rivals. . . . None.
I swear by all that's holy, any rivals, I will kill them.

(Natásha crosses the room with a candle.)

NATASHA *(Glancing in at one door, then another, and passing the door to her husband's room)*: Andréi. . . . Oh, let him read. *(Sees Solyóny)* Oh! Excuse me, Vassíly Vassílich, I didn't know you were here, I'm not dressed . . .

SOLYONY: What difference does that make? Goodnight. *(Leaves)*

NATASHA: Irína, you're all worn out, you poor thing! *(Kisses Irína)* You shouldn't stay up so late.

IRINA: Is Bobik asleep?

NATASHA: Yes. But not very well. By the way, I wanted to tell you before but you weren't here, or I never had time. I think Bobik's room is too cold and damp, where he is now, I mean. And your room is exactly right for a baby's room. You just move in with Ólga for a while, dear, that's a good girl.

IRINA *(Not understanding)*: What?

(The sound of sleigh bells outside.)

NATASHA: You and Ólga will have one room, and Bobik goes in your room. Just for a while. He's such a darlin', this morning I said to him, "Bobik," I said, "You're mine! All mine!" And he just looked at me with those big eyes of his.

(The doorbell rings.)

That must be Ólga. She's so late!

(The maid comes in and whispers something in Natásha's ear.)

Protopópov? What a crazy man! Protopópov is
outside, he wants me to go for a sleigh ride with him.
(Laughs) Men are so funny. . . . Well, maybe just a
little one, fifteen minutes or so . . . *(To the maid)* Tell
him I'll be right out.

(The doorbell.)

Now who is it? Well, that must be Ólga.

*(She leaves. The maid hurries out; Irína sits thinking. Enter
Kulýgin, Ólga, and behind them Vershínin.)*

KULYGIN: Now how do you like that. And they said they
were having a party.

VERSHININ: That's funny, I only left about a half an hour
ago, and they were waiting for the carnival people.

IRINA: Everybody left.

KULYGIN: Did Másha leave? Where did she go? And why
is Protopópov waiting outside? Who's he waiting for?

IRINA: Oh, stop bothering me! I'm worn out!

KULYGIN: Well, Miss High and Mighty!

OLGA: The meeting just ended. I'm in agony. Our
headmistress is sick and I have to substitute for her.
And my head, my head is aching so . . . *(Sits down)*
Andréi lost two hundred rubles playing cards last
night. . . . The whole town is talking about it . . .

KULYGIN: Yes, even I got tired at that meeting. *(Sits
down)*

VERSHININ: My wife tried to kill herself again, but she
was just trying to throw a scare into me. She's out of
danger now, and I feel better. But, I suppose that

means we should go. Well, I wish you all a very good
night. Fyódor Ilých, let's go out somewhere! I really
can't go home right now—what do you say?

KULYGIN: I'm tired, I can't. *(Stands)* I'm tired. Did my
wife go home?

IRINA: Probably.

KULYGIN *(Kisses Irina's hand)*: Goodbye. Tomorrow and
the day after are holidays. Have a pleasant rest! *(Goes)*
I would dearly love a cup of tea. I'd been counting on
spending an evening with entertaining company . . .
well. . . . *O, fallacem hominum spem!* Accusative of
exclamation.

VERSHININ: All right, I'll go by myself.

(He leaves with Kulygin, whistling.)

OLGA: My head aches so. Andréi lost . . . the whole town
is talking . . . I'm going to bed. *(Starts off)* I've got
the day off tomorrow. . . . Oh God, how pleasant!
Tomorrow off, and the day after too. . . . But my
head aches so. *(Leaves)*

IRINA: They've all gone. There's no one left.

*(Out in the street someone is playing an accordion. The nurse
sings. Natásha crosses the room in a fur coat and hat; the maid
follows her.)*

NATASHA: I'll be back in half an hour. I'm only going for
a little ride. *(Leaves)*

IRINA *(Alone, longing)*: I want to go to Moscow! Moscow!
Moscow!

CURTAIN

Act Three

Ólga and Irína's room. Beds right and left, behind screens. It is after two in the morning. Fire alarms are heard in the distance; they have been going for some time and it's obvious that no one in the house has been to bed yet. Másha lies on the sofa, dressed in black as usual.

Enter Ólga and Anfisa.

ANFISA: They're sitting downstairs in the hallway right now . . . I told them to come on up, "Come on up," I said, "You can't just sit there like that." And they're crying their eyes out, "We don't know what happened to Papa," they said, "maybe he got burnt up." Can you believe it? And there's some more people out in the yard, they don't hardly have any clothes on either . . .

OLGA *(Taking a dress out of the closet)*: Nana, take that gray one . . . and that one too . . . and the blouse too . . . and take this skirt, Nana. . . . What a terrible thing, my God! The whole of Kirsanov street must have burned. . . . Take this one . . . and this. *(Piles dresses*

on Anfisa's arms) The poor Vershínins got an awful
scare, their house nearly burned down. They can
spend the night with us, we can't just let them go
home. And poor Fedótik lost everything, his place
burned to the ground . . .

ANFISA: Olga dear, you better get Ferapónt. I'll never
manage all this myself.

OLGA: Who's down there? Ferapónt, come up here, will
you?

*(Outside the windows the sky is red from the fire; fire engines
are heard going by the house.)*

OLGA: What a nightmare all this is. And how tired of it
all I am.

(Enter Ferapónt.)

Here take this stuff, take it downstairs. The Kolotílin
girls are in the hallway, give it to them . . . wait, give
them this, too.

FERAPONT: All right. Moscow burnt down too, long time
ago. Them Frenchies sure got a surprise.

OLGA: Go on, go on, get out . . .

FERAPONT: All right, I'm goin' . . .

OLGA: Nana dear, give it all away. We don't need any of
it, Nana, give it all away. . . . I'm so tired I can
hardly stand. . . . We can't let the Vershínins go home.
The girls can sleep in the living room, the Colonel
can stay with the Baron, Fedótik can stay with the
Baron too, or maybe someplace downstairs. The
Doctor is drunk again, dead drunk, wouldn't you
know it, so we can't put anyone in with him. And
Vershínin's wife can go in the living room too.

ANFISA *(Breaking with fatigue)*: Ólga dear, Ólyushka, don't send me away, please! Please don't!

OLGA: Don't talk nonsense, Nana. Nobody's going to send you away.

ANFISA *(Leaning against Ólga)*: My little girl, my little darling, I do what I can, I work all the time. . . . I know I'm not what I used to be, everybody says send her away, but where am I supposed to go? Where? I'm old, I'm old, I'm old . . .

OLGA: Nana, why don't you sit down. . . . Poor love, you're worn out! *(Helps her sit down)* You just rest, darling. You're so pale!

(Natásha enters.)

NATASHA: They're saying we better get a group together to organize aid for the people who got burnt out. It's a lovely idea, don't you think? We should help out the poor anyway, that's one of your responsibilities if you're rich. Bobik and little Sophie are fast asleep, they're sleeping as if nothing in the world were going on. And we've got so many people, everywhere you look the house is full of them. There's some kind of flu going around, I'm scared the children will catch it.

OLGA *(Not listening to her)*: You really can't see the fire from this room, it's quieter here.

NATASHA: Yes . . . I must be a mess. *(Looks in the mirror)* Who said I was putting on weight? It's not true! Not a bit! And Másha's asleep, she must be worn out, poor thing . . . *(To Anfisa, coldly)* Don't you dare sit down when I'm around! Get up! And get out of here!

(Anfisa goes out; pause.)

Why you keep that old woman around I will never understand.

OLGA *(Stunned)*: Excuse me, I don't understand either . . .

NATASHA: You just spoil her! She doesn't do a thing! She's a peasant, she should be living on a farm. I like things nice and neat around the house, I don't want things sloppy! *(Pats Ólga's cheek)* Poor sweet thing, you're tired! Our headmistress is all tired out! When my little Sophie grows up and starts high school, I'll have to start being scared of you.

OLGA: I'm not going to be headmistress.

NATASHA: Yes you are, Ólga. It's all settled.

OLGA: I refuse. I can't, I just don't have the strength for it. *(Takes a drink of water)* You were so rude to Nana just now. . . . Forgive me, I'm in no condition for scenes like that . . . I'm even a little faint . . .

NATASHA *(Upset)*: I'm sorry, Ólga, I'm sorry. I didn't mean to upset you.

(Másha gets up, takes her pillow and leaves, angrily.)

OLGA: Dear, you have got to understand. We may have been brought up rather differently, still I . . . I can't bear scenes like that. I get depressed when I see someone treated like that, I get physically *sick*. . . . Really, I . . . my strength just goes . . .

NATASHA: I'm sorry, I'm really sorry . . . *(Kisses her)*

OLGA: The least little vulgarity, an indelicate expression, and I get terribly upset . . .

NATASHA: I know I say things I shouldn't, dear, I know, but you have to agree she could go live on a farm.

OLGA: But she's been with us for thirty years!

NATASHA: But she can't do any work anymore! Either I

don't understand you, or you don't want to
understand me. She *cannot work*, she just sits around
or she sleeps.

OLGA: Then let her sleep.

NATASHA *(Astonished)*: What do you mean, let her sleep?
She's a servant, isn't she? *(Almost crying)* I just don't
understand you, Ólga. I have two nurses for the
children, we have a maid and a cook. . . . What do we
need that old woman for? What for?

(Fire alarms in the distance.)

OLGA: I think I've aged ten years tonight.

NATASHA: We've got to come to some agreement, Ólga.
Once and for all. You're at the high school, I'm at
home. Your job is teaching, mine is running this
house. And if I tell you something about the servants,
then I know what I'm talking about. I know what *I
am talk-ing a-bout!* And I don't want to see that stupid
old woman around here tomorrow! *(Stamps her foot)*
And don't you dare argue with me! Don't you dare!
(Calms down a little) Really, if you don't move down
to the basement apartment we are always going to be
fighting like this. It's terrible.

(Enter Kulýgin.)

KULYGIN: Where's Másha? We should have gone home
long ago. They say the fire's dying down. *(Yawns and
stretches)* They only lost one block but it was so
windy, at first they thought the whole town would
burn down. *(Sits down)* I'm tired. Ólga dearest . . . I
sometimes think if I hadn't married Másha I would

have married you, Ólga. You're a wonderful woman . . . I'm so tired. *(Listens for a bit)*

OLGA: What's the matter?

KULYGIN: The doctor's been drinking, wouldn't you
know. He's extremely drunk. Wouldn't you know!
(Gets up) I think he's coming up here. . . . Do you
hear him? Yes, here he comes . . . *(Laughs)* What a
character, really . . . I'm going to hide. *(Goes behind a
screen in the corner)* The old joker.

OLGA: He hasn't had a drop in two years, and all of a
sudden he starts in again . . .

*(Ólga goes upstage with Natásha. Chebutýkin enters; he walks
straight as if he were sober, crosses the room, stops, looks around,
goes over to the washstand and starts to wash his hands.)*

CHEBUTYKIN *(Sullen)*: The hell with 'em all . . . the hell
with 'em. They think I'm a doctor and I know how to
cure people but I don't know anything. I forgot
everything I knew, I don't remember a thing. Not a
thing.

(Ólga and Natásha go out; he doesn't notice.)

The hell with 'em. Last Wednesday I went out to
Zasyp to take care of a sick woman. She died, and it's
my fault she died. My fault. . . . Maybe I knew
something twenty-five years ago, but now I can't
remember a thing. My head is empty, and so is my
heart. Maybe I'm not even human. . . . Maybe I don't
even exist, maybe it's all my imagination . . . *(Starts
to cry)* Oh, I wish I didn't exist! *(Stops crying. Sullen,
as before)* What the hell. . . . Two days ago I went to
the club, they were all talking about Shakespeare and

Voltaire, I never read 'em, but I pretended like I did.
So did all the rest of 'em. They all pretended. Made
me sick! I kept thinking about that woman who died
on Wednesday, I kept thinking about everything, and
I got feeling ugly and twisted and mean. . . . So I
went out and got drunk.

*(Irína, Vershínin and Túzenbach enter; Túzenbach has on
brand-new civilian clothes, very stylish.)*

IRINA: Come in and sit down. Nobody will bother us here.
VERSHININ: If it weren't for the troops the whole town
    would have burned! Terrific, every one of them! *(Rubs
    his hands with satisfaction)* Good boys! Just terrific!
KULYGIN *(Coming out from behind the screen)*: Does
    anybody know what time it is?
TUZENBACH: It's already after three. It's getting light.
IRINA: Everybody's just sitting around downstairs, nobody
    wants to leave. Even that Solyóny of yours is down
    there . . . *(To Chebutýkin)* Doctor, you ought to go to
    bed.
CHEBUTYKIN: S'all right. Thanks a lot. *(Combs his beard)*
KULYGIN *(Laughing)*: You've been at the bottle, Iván
    Románich. *(Slaps him on the back)* Congratulations! *In
    vino veritas*, the ancients used to say.
TUZENBACH: They've been after me to organize a benefit
    concert for the people who were burnt out.
IRINA: Here? Who could you get?
TUZENBACH: We could do it if we really wanted to. María
    Sergéyevna, for instance. She plays the piano beau-
    tifully.
KULYGIN: Beautifully!

IRINA: She forgot how long ago. She hasn't played in three years . . . maybe four.

TUZENBACH: Nobody in this town understands music, not a single soul, but I do, and I tell you she has talent.

KULYGIN: You're right, Baron. I love Másha a great deal. She's a splendid woman.

TUZENBACH: Can you imagine what it must be like, to play so beautifully and to realize that there is no one, no one who understands you!

KULYGIN *(Sighing)*: Yes. . . . But would it be proper for her to perform in public? *(Pause)* Of course, I really know nothing about it. It might be perfectly all right. But you have to remember that our headmaster has rather particular views—he's a fine man, a very fine man, very intelligent. . . . I suppose it's not really his business, but still—if you want I could probably have a talk with him.

(Chebutýkin picks up a porcelain clock and examines it.)

VERSHININ: I'm a mess. I got terribly dirty at the fire. *(Pause)* I heard a rumor the other day, something about our brigade being transferred. Maybe to Poland, maybe to the Chinese border, nobody knows.

TUZENBACH: That's what I heard too. Well, that will empty out the town.

IRINA: And we're leaving too!

(Chebutýkin drops the clock and it smashes to pieces.)

CHEBUTYKIN: Smash!

(Pause; everyone is distressed and upset.)

KULYGIN *(Picking up the pieces)*: Iván Románich, Iván
  Románich, such an expensive clock, and you broke it!
  You get an F-minus in conduct!

IRINA: That was mama's clock.

CHEBUTYKIN: Maybe. Mama's. All right, so it was
  mama's. Maybe I didn't even break it. Maybe it just
  looks like it's broken. Maybe we don't even exist,
  maybe it just looks like it. I don't know anything, and
  nobody else knows anything either. *(At the door)* What
  are you all looking at? Natásha's having a little affair
  with Protopópov, but you can't see that. You just sit
  there and you can't see that Natásha is having a little
  affair with Protopópov. *(Sings)* "Don't you like this
  little fig I'm giving you . . ." *(Leaves)*

VERSHININ: Well . . . *(Laughs)* This is all really very
  strange, isn't it? *(Pause)* When the fire started I ran
  right home; as soon as I got there I realized our house
  was safe and sound, but my two little girls were
  standing in the doorway, all they had on was their
  underwear, their mother was gone, there were people
  running everywhere, horses, dogs barking, and on
  those little girls' faces was a look of horror, fear,
  anxiety, I don't know what all, it wrung my heart to
  see them like that. My God, I thought, what will
  those little girls have to go through during their
  lifetime! I picked them up and brought them here, but
  all I could think of was what they would have to go
  through before they die.

(Fire sirens; pause.)

And when I got here, I found their mother—angry,
screaming.

(Másha enters, carrying her pillow; she sits down on the sofa.)

And when my little girls were standing there in their underwear, with no shoes on, and the street was all red from the fire, and the noise was terrible, I thought: this is the way things used to happen years ago—a surprise enemy attack, arson and looting. . . . And yet of course there's really an enormous difference between then and now, isn't there? And after a little time goes by, say, two or three hundred years, people will look back on our life with horror, or they'll laugh, and the things we do today will seem strange and complicated and impractical. And oh, what a life that will be then! *(Laughs)* Excuse me, I'm talking too much again, it's just the mood I'm in. *(Pause)* You're all asleep. Well, I'll keep talking anyway. What a life that will be! Just think: right now there are only three people like you in this town, another generation and there will be more, and then more and more, and a time will come when the whole world will have changed because of you, and everyone will live like you do, and finally even you will become part of the past, and people will be born who are better than you . . . *(Laughs)* I'm in the strangest mood today. I feel an urge to live, to do something wild! *(Sings) Lyubov vse vosrasty pokorny, yeyo poryvy blagotvorny . . . (Laughs)*

MASHA: *Tram-tam-tam . . .*

VERSHININ: *Tram-tam . . .*

MASHA: *Tra-ra-ra?*

VERSHININ: *Tra-ta-ta. (Laughs)*

(Enter Fedótik.)

FEDOTIK *(Dancing)*: It's all burnt up! Everything's gone! It's all burnt up!

(Laughter.)

IRINA: What's so funny about it? Is everything burnt?
FEDOTIK: Everything. It's all gone. The guitar burned and the camera burned and all my letters burned. . . . And I bought a little notebook for you, and that burned too . . .

(Enter Solyóny.)

IRINA: No, please, Vassíly Vassílich, go away! You can't come in here!
SOLYONY: How come the Baron can and I can't?
VERSHININ: We should all go, in fact. How's the fire?
SOLYONY: They said it's stopped. Now I find that extremely funny, that the Baron can come in here and I can't. *(Takes out his cologne bottle and rubs some on his hands)*
VERSHININ: *Tram-tam-tam.*
MASHA: *Tram-tam.*
VERSHININ *(Laughing; to Solyóny)*: Let's go downstairs.
SOLYONY: Very well. We'll just make a little note of this. *(Looking at Túzenbach)* Wee, wee, wee, wee . . .

(He goes out with Vershínin and Fedótik.)

IRINA: That Solyóny has gotten the place all smelly . . . *(Surprised)* The Baron's asleep! Baron! Baron!
TUZENBACH *(Opening his eyes)*: I was tireder than I thought . . . a brick factory. . . . Actually it's not a dream, I'll be starting work soon at a brick factory.

I've already had an interview with them. *(To Irína, tenderly)* You're so pale and beautiful . . . you're fascinating. . . . Your paleness lights up the dark . . . you're sad, you're unhappy with life, oh, come away with me, let's go off and work together!

MASHA: Nikolái Lvóvich, will you please get out?

TUZENBACH *(Laughing)*: Are you here? I didn't see you. *(Kisses Irína's hand)* Goodbye, I'm going. . . . When I look at you now, Irína, I remember a while back, on your birthday, how alive you were, laughing and talking about going to work. . . . What a happy life I dreamed of then—and where is it? *(Kisses her hand)* You have tears in your eyes. Go to bed, it's already daylight . . . it's morning. . . . Oh, if only I could sacrifice my life for you!

MASHA: Nikolái Lvóvich, get out! Really, you are the limit . . .

TUZENBACH: I'm going. *(Leaves)*

MASHA *(Lying down)*: Are you asleep, Fyódor?

KULYGIN: What?

MASHA: You should go home.

KULYGIN: Másha dearest, my sweet Másha . . .

IRINA: She's worn out, Fyódor. Let her get some rest.

KULYGIN: I'm going right now. . . . My dear wife, my wonderful wife . . . I love you, my only . . .

MASHA *(Angrily)*: Amo, amas, amat, amamus, amatis, amant.

KULYGIN *(Laughing)*: Isn't she astonishing! I've been married to you for seven years, and it seems like only yesterday. No, truly, you're astonishing. And I'm happy. I'm a happy, happy man!

MASHA: And I'm bored. I am bored, bored, bored! *(Straightens up and speaks sitting there)* There's one thing I can't get out of my head, it feels like someone

nailed it there. I mean Andréi—he took out a
mortgage on this house, and his wife got all the
money, and this house isn't just his, it belongs to the
four of us! He must know that, if he's got any decency
left.

KULYGIN: Why bring it up, Másha? It doesn't affect you.
Andréi owes money all over town, I feel sorry for him.

MASHA: I don't care, it's still revolting. *(Lies down)*

KULYGIN: You and I are not poor. I work, I teach at the
high school, I give private lessons in my spare
time . . . I'm a plain, honest man. *Omnia mea mecum
porto*, as they say.

MASHA: I don't want anything, but the injustice of it
revolts me. *(Pause)* Go on home, Fyódor.

KULYGIN *(Kissing her)*: You're tired, you take a little rest,
I'll wait downstairs for you. Get some sleep . . .
(Crosses to the door) I'm a happy, happy man. *(Goes
out)*

IRINA: Andréi has gotten so petty, so slow and so old
living with that woman. He used to want to be a
scientist, and yesterday he was bragging that he'd
finally become a member of the county council. He's a
member, and Protopópov is the chairman. . . . The
whole town is talking and laughing, and he's the only
one who doesn't know anything, doesn't see anything.
Tonight everybody went to see the fire, but not him.
He just sits in his room and pays no attention to
anything, he just plays his violin. *(On edge)* Oh, it's
awful, it's awful, awful! *(Cries)* I can't stand it. I can't
stand it anymore! I can't, I can't!

*(Ólga enters and goes to straighten up her dressing table. Irína
sobs loudly.)*

Throw me out, please, get rid of me! I can't stand it
anymore!

OLGA *(Frightened)*: What's the matter? Darling, what's the
matter?

IRINA *(Sobbing)*: Where is it? Where did it all go? Oh, my
God, my God! I've forgotten everything . . . my head
is all mixed up . . . I can't remember the Italian word
for window, or ceiling. . . . I keep forgetting things,
every day I forget more and more and life goes by and
it won't ever come back and we're never going to
Moscow, never, never, I can see it all now, we're never
going to get there . . . *(Trying to control herself)* Oh,
I'm so unhappy . . . I can't work anymore, I won't
work anymore. I'm sick of it, I've had enough! I
worked at the telegraph office and now I work at the
municipal building and I despise it, I hate everything
I have to do there. . . . I'm almost twenty-four, I've
been working all this time and my brain has shrivelled
up, I've lost my looks, I've gotten old, and nothing,
nothing! There's no satisfaction in any of it and the
time passes and you realize you'll never have the
beautiful life you dreamed of, you just keep digging
yourself deeper and deeper into a hole. . . . I'm in
despair, I am really in despair! And I don't understand why I'm still alive, I should have killed myself
long ago.

OLGA: Don't cry, my little girl, don't cry. . . . It tears me
apart.

IRINA: I'm not crying, I'm not. . . . It's all right. . . .
There, see, I'm not crying anymore. It's all right, it's
all right!

OLGA: Dearest, let me talk to you, as your sister, as a
friend. If you want my advice, marry the Baron.

(Irína weeps quietly.)

After all, you respect him, you value his friend-
ship. . . . I know, he's not very good-looking, but he's
a good man, an honest man. . . . People don't marry
for love, they marry because they're supposed to. At
least I think they do. I would have married without
love. It wouldn't have made any difference who it was,
as long as he was an honest man. I'd even marry an
old man . . .

IRINA: I kept waiting for us to move to Moscow, I knew
I'd meet my true love there, I used to dream about
him. But you see it was all a lot of nonsense . . .

OLGA *(Hugging her sister)*: Oh darling, I know, I know;
when the Baron resigned from the service and first
came to see us in his civilian clothes, he was so plain-
looking I started to cry. . . . And he asked me what I
was crying about, and what could I tell him? But if
God brings the two of you together, I would be very
happy. You see, things are very different from what
you thought, very different.

*(Natásha enters with a candle in her hand. She walks silently
across the room in a straight line from right to left.)*

MASHA *(Sitting)*: You'd think she started the fire herself /cun
                                                              /decendn
OLGA: Másha, you are so silly. . . . You are the silliest
person in this family! . . . I'm sorry, excuse me.

(Pause.)

MASHA: My dear sisters, I want to confess something. I
want to bare my soul. I want to confess something to
you and then I never want to say another word about

it ever again. I want to tell you everything right now.
(Quietly) It's my secret, but you should know it any-
way . . . I can't keep it to myself anymore . . . *(Pause)*
I'm in love, I'm in love . . . I love that man . . . the
one you saw just now. . . . Well, that's it . . . I love
Vershínin.

OLGA *(Going behind the screen to her bed)*: Stop that, I'm
not going to listen.

MASHA: What can I do! *(Puts her hands to her head)* At
first I thought he was strange, then I started feeling
sorry for him . . . then I fell in love with him . . . in
love with his voice, with the things he says, with all
his problems, with his two little girls . . .

OLGA *(Behind the screen)*: I'm not listening, I don't care
what you're saying, I'm not listening.

MASHA: Oh, Ólga, you're the silly one. I'm in love! It's
fate, I guess—I mean it's just my luck. And he loves
me. . . . It's all so funny. Don't you think so? Doesn't
it strike you funny? *(Takes Irína's hand, draws her close)*
Oh, my darling, we'll get through life somehow, no
matter what happens to us. . . . When you read about
these things in books it all seems terribly silly and
predictable, but when you fall in love yourself you
realize nobody knows anything about it, everyone has
to figure it out for herself. My dear sisters, there. I've
told you. Now I will never say another word about it.
The rest is silence.

(Enter Andréi, then Ferapónt.)

ANDREI: What is it you want? I don't understand . . .

FERAPONT *(At the door, impatient)*: Andréi Sergéyich, I
already told you ten times.

ANDREI: In the first place, when you speak to me, you call
       me sir, and not Andréi Sergéyich.
FERAPONT: Sir. The firemen want to know can they go
       through the yard to get to the river, they can't keep
       goin' around and around like they been.
ANDREI: All right! Tell them all right.

(Ferapónt leaves.)

What a bore. Where's Ólga?

(Ólga motions from behind the screen.)

I came to ask you for a key to the cupboard. I lost
mine. I know you've got that little one.

*(Ólga gives him a key in silence. Irína goes behind her screen;
pause.)*

What a terrible fire! It seems to be dying down. That
damn Ferapónt made me so mad, I didn't know how
silly I sounded. . . . "Sir . . ." *(Pause)* Why don't you
say anything, Ólga? *(Pause)* Look, it's time you
stopped this nonsense, all this sulking for no reason.
You and Másha are here, Irína's here, fine, let's get this
out in the open once and for all. What is it you all
have against me? Hunh?
OLGA: Not now, Andréi. We can talk tomorrow. *(Shaking)*
       What an awful night!
ANDREI *(Terribly embarrassed)*: Don't get upset. I just want
       to know very calmly what it is you all have against
       me. Just tell me.

(Vershínin's voice: "Tram-tam-tam.")

MASHA *(Standing; loudly)*: *Tra-ta-ta!* *(To Ólga)* Goodbye, Ólga, God bless you. *(Goes behind the screen and kisses Irína)* Sleep well. Goodbye, Andréi. Leave them alone, they're exhausted. We can talk tomorrow. *(Leaves)*

OLGA: Please, Andréi. Let it go until tomorrow . . . *(Goes behind her screen)* It's time to go to bed.

ANDREI: No, I'm going to say what I came for and then I'll go. Right this minute. In the first place, you've got something against my wife Natásha, and I've noticed it since the day I got married. Natásha is a lovely person, honest and straightforward and well brought-up. In my opinion. I love my wife and I respect her, you understand? I respect her and I want to make sure the rest of you respect her too. I repeat, she is a lovely person, and all your remarks and attitudes— well, excuse me, but you're just being stuck up . . . *(Pause)* In the second place, you all seem mad at me because I'm not a scientist or a professor or something. But I have an occupation, I'm a member of the county council, and I consider that just as honorable and just as important as an intellectual career. I'm a member of the county council and I'm proud of it, if you want to know . . . *(Pause)* In the third place . . . I still have something more to say . . . I mortgaged this house, and I didn't get your permission. It's my fault and I'm sorry and I ask you to forgive me. I had to do it because I owed a lot of money—thirty-five thousand. I don't gamble anymore, I gave it up, but the main thing is you're all girls, you get a military pension, and I don't! I don't have any income at all . . .

(Pause.)

KULYGIN *(At the door)*: Isn't Másha here? *(Nervously)*
　　Where is she? That's funny . . . *(Leaves)*
ANDREI: You're not listening. Natásha is a fine, honest
　　woman. *(Walks up and down in silence, then stops)* When
　　I got married, I thought that we'd all live happily
　　together . . . happily. . . . But oh my God . . . *(Starts
　　to cry)* Oh, my dear sisters, my darling sisters, don't
　　believe me, don't believe me . . . *(Leaves)*
KULYGIN *(At the door, nervously)*: Where's Másha? Isn't
　　she here? This is very disturbing.

(He leaves. Sirens. The stage is empty.)

IRINA: Ólga! Somebody's knocking.
OLGA: It's the Doctor. He's drunk.
IRINA: What an awful night! *(Pause)* Ólga, *(Glances from
　　behind the screen)* did you hear the news? The Brigade
　　is leaving. They're being transferred someplace far
　　away.
OLGA: That's just a rumor.
IRINA: We'll be left here all alone . . . Ólga!
OLGA: What?
IRINA: Ólga dear, I do respect the Baron, I do, he's a
　　wonderful man, I will marry him, I promise, only
　　please let's go to Moscow! I beg you, please! There's
　　no place in the world like Moscow! Let's go, Ólga!
　　Please!

CURTAIN

Act Four

The old garden of the Prózorov house. A long walk lined with fir trees, leading to the river. Across the river is a forest. At the right is the porch of the house; a table with a bottle and glasses. They have just been drinking champagne. It is noon. People occasionally walk through the garden toward the river. A group of five soldiers crosses in a hurry.

Chebutýkin is in good spirits; he remains so for the duration of the act. He sits in a chair in the garden, waiting for someone to send for him; he wears a cap and carries a stick. Irína, Kulýgin, wearing a decoration and with his moustache shaved off, and Túzenbach stand on the porch, saying goodbye to Fedótik and Róhde, who are coming down the steps; both officers are in field uniform.

TUZENBACH *(Hugging Fedótik)*: You're a good friend; we had good times together. *(Hugs Róhde)* Once more. . . . Goodbye, Róhde!

IRINA: Till we meet again!

FEDOTIK: No, this time it's goodbye forever, we'll never see each other again!

KULYGIN: Who knows? *(Wipes his eyes and smiles)* Even I'm starting to cry.

IRINA: We may meet again sometime.

FEDOTIK: What, in ten or fifteen years? But we won't hardly recognize each other, and we'll be very nervous and embarrassed. *(Takes a picture)* Hold it! Just one more time.

ROHDE *(Hugging Túzenbach)*: No, we'll never see each other again . . . *(Kisses Irína's hand)* Thank you for everything, thank you so much!

FEDOTIK *(Vexed)*: Oh, just hold on a minute!

TUZENBACH: I hope we do meet again. But you be sure and write us, don't forget.

ROHDE *(Looking around the garden)*: Goodbye, trees! *(Shouts)* Hey! Hey! *(Pause)* Goodbye, echo!

KULYGIN: Who knows? Maybe if you're lucky you'll get married there in Poland. . . . You get a Polish wife, they kiss you all the time and call you "Kokhany." *(Laughs)*

FEDOTIK *(Looking at his watch)*: We've got less than an hour. Solyóny's the only one from our battery going on the barge, the rest of us go with the men. There are three batteries going today and three more tomorrow—and after that peace and quiet will settle down upon the place once again.

TUZENBACH: As well as godawful boredom.

ROHDE: Where's María Sergéyevna?

KULYGIN: Másha's somewhere out here in the garden.

FEDOTIK: I've got to say goodbye to her.

ROHDE: Goodbye, I'd better go, otherwise I'll start crying. *(Hugs Túzenbach and Kulýgin and kisses Irína's hand)* We had such a wonderful time here . . .

FEDOTIK *(To Kulýgin)*: Here's a little souvenir . . . a little

book with a little pencil attached. . . . We'll go this
way, down by the river . . .

(They go off through the trees, looking around as they go.)

ROHDE *(Shouting)*: Hey! Hey! Hey-ay!
KULYGIN *(Shouting)*: Goodbye!

*(In the garden Fedótik and Róhde meet Másha and say good-
bye; she goes off with them.)*

IRINA: They're gone . . . *(Sits down on the lowest step)*
CHEBUTYKIN: They forgot to say goodbye to me.
IRINA: Why didn't you say goodbye to them?
CHEBUTYKIN: I must have forgot. Anyway I'll see them
    two days from now; I'm leaving tomorrow.
    Hmm . . . only one day left. But next year I retire,
    and then I'll come back here and spend the rest of my
    days with you. Just one more year, and I get my
    pension . . . *(Puts one newspaper in his pocket and takes
    out another)* I'll come back here and reform my life.
    I'll be so reserved, so re . . . so respectable, a real
    model of retirement.
IRINA: You certainly ought to reform your life, my dear.
    Anything would help.
CHEBUTYKIN: You're right. I think so too. *(Sings softly)*
    Tara-ra-boom-der-ay, it's gonna rain today . . .
KULYGIN: Iván Románich, you're unreformable!
    Unreformable!
CHEBUTYKIN: Maybe I should take lessons from you.
    Then I'd do better, eh?
IRINA: Fyódor shaved his moustache off. I can't bear it.
KULYGIN: So?

CHEBUTYKIN: I could tell you what your face looks like now, but I won't.

KULYGIN: What do you mean? It's perfectly normal, a *modus vivendi*. Our headmaster shaved his moustache, so when I was promoted I shaved mine. Nobody likes it, but that makes no difference to me whatsoever. I'm quite happy. With a moustache or without a moustache, I am still a happy man.

(He sits down. Upstage, Andréi wheels a baby carriage.)

IRINA: Iván Románich dear, I'm really worried. What happened yesterday on the boulevard?

CHEBUTYKIN: What happened? Nothing. Just a lot of nonsense. *(Reads his paper)* What difference does it make?

KULYGIN: What *I* heard was, Solyóny and the Baron met on the boulevard near the theatre . . .

TUZENBACH: Please! That's enough, for godssakes . . .

(Makes a gesture of impatience and goes into the house)

KULYGIN: . . . near the theatre, and Solyóny started teasing the Baron, and he couldn't take it anymore and said something insulting . . .

CHEBUTYKIN: I don't know anything about it. It's all a lot of nonsense.

KULYGIN: . . . and they say that Solyóny is in love with Irína and that's why he can't stand the Baron. Well, it's understandable. Irína's a wonderful girl. She's very much like my Másha, both very thoughtful. Only your personality is easier, Irína. Of course Másha has a very good personality too. I love her, I really do.

(From the garden backstage: Hey! Hey! Yoo-hoo!)

IRINA *(Shivering)*: Everything scares me today. *(Pause)*
I'm all ready to leave, I just have to finish packing
after lunch. The Baron and I are getting married
tomorrow, and then we go away to the brick factory,
and the day after I start teaching, and that's when our
new life begins. God, I hope it all works out! When I
passed the exams for my teaching certificate, I
practically cried . . . *(Pause)* The cart is coming to
pick up my things . . .

KULYGIN: Well, I suppose you're doing the right thing,
but somehow it doesn't seem all that serious to me.
It's just a lot of ideas, not much practice. Anyway, I
wish you all the best, sincerely I do.

CHEBUTYKIN *(Tenderly)*: My dear, my little darling. . . .
You've all gone so far ahead of me I'll never catch up.
I'll stay right here, left behind like a migrating bird
that's too old to fly. You fly, sweetheart, you fly!
(Pause) Fyodor Ilých, you should never have shaved
off your moustache.

KULYGIN: That's enough out of you. *(Sighs)* Well, the
troops are leaving today, and then everything will be
back the way it used to be. Whatever people say,
Másha is a wonderful woman, an honest woman, I
love her and thank God for her. People turn out
differently. . . . There's a clerk in the local tax office,
Kózyrev, his name is, we went to high school
together. He never graduated because he couldn't
understand the *ut consecutivum* construction. He's
terribly poor, not well at all, and whenever I see him I
say: "Hello there, *ut consecutivum*! "Yes," he says, "*ut
consecutivum*, that's right," and then he coughs. I've
been lucky all my life, I'm happy, I've even got a
certificate of merit and now I teach the *ut consecutivum*

to others. Of course, I'm intelligent, more intelligent than most, but that won't necessarily make you happy . . .

(Inside the house someone is playing "The Maiden's Prayer.")

IRINA: And tomorrow evening I won't ever have to hear her play that "Maiden's Prayer" again, I'll never see Protopópov again . . . *(Pause)* Protopópov is sitting right there in the living room; he even showed up today . . .

KULYGIN: Has the headmistress gotten home yet?

(In the distance, Másha walks slowly in the garden.)

IRINA: No. We sent for her. If you only knew how hard it's been for me, living here alone without Ólga, now that she has an apartment near the high school. She's headmistress and she's busy all day long, and I'm here by myself; I have nothing to do, I'm bored and I hate that room I'm in. . . . I made up my mind: if I can't go to Moscow, then that's the way it has to be, it's fate. There's nothing you can do about it. . . . Nikolái Lvóvich proposed to me, and I accepted. He's a good man, it's surprising how good he is. And all of a sudden I felt happy, less depressed, and I felt like working again. Only last night something happened, nobody will tell me what, but I feel uneasy about it. . . .

CHEBUTYKIN: Nothing happened. Just a lot of nonsense.

NATASHA *(At the window)*: The headmistress is here!

KULYGIN: Here's the headmistress. Let's go.

(He and Irína go into the house.)

CHEBUTYKIN *(Reading his paper and singing softly)*: Tara-ra-boom-der-ay, it's gonna rain today . . .

(Másha comes up; in the distance Andréi wheels the baby carriage.)

MASHA: He sits there, he just sits and sits . . .

CHEBUTYKIN: So what?

MASHA *(Sitting down)*: Nothing. *(Pause)* Did you love my mother?

CHEBUTYKIN: Very much.

MASHA: Did she love you?

CHEBUTYKIN *(After a pause)*: That I can't remember.

MASHA: Where's my man? That's the way our old cook Martha used to talk about her policeman: "My man." Where's my man?

CHEBUTYKIN: He's not here yet.

MASHA: When you only get your happiness in bits and pieces and then lose it anyway, like me, you begin to get bitter about it. You don't care what you say anymore. *(Touches her breast)* I'm full of anger inside.

(Looks at Andréi, who pushes the baby carriage toward them.)

Look at our little brother Andréi, all his hopes are gone. A thousand people raise a bell, they spend all kinds of money and effort, and all of a sudden it falls and goes smash. All of a sudden. Nobody's fault. Just like Andréi.

ANDREI: I wish they'd quiet down in there. What a racket.

CHEBUTYKIN: Won't be long now. *(Takes out his watch; he winds it and it strikes)* I've got an old-fashioned watch; it strikes. The first and second and fifth batteries all leave exactly at one. *(Pause)* And I leave tomorrow.

ANDREI: For good?

CHEBUTYKIN: I don't know. Maybe I'll come back next year. Who the hell knows. . . . And what difference does it make?

(Somewhere in the distance, street musicians are playing a harp and violin.)

ANDREI: The town's almost empty. It seems to be falling asleep . . . *(Pause)* What happened by the theatre yesterday? Everybody's talking about it, and I don't know a thing.

CHEBUTYKIN: Nothing. It's all a lot of nonsense. Solyóny started teasing the Baron, and he lost his temper and insulted Solyóny, and the way it wound up Solyóny had to challenge him to a duel. *(Looks at his watch)* It ought to be about time now . . . twelve-thirty in the state forest across the river—you can see it from here. Bang-bang. *(Laughs)* Solyóny thinks he's Lérmontov, he even writes poetry. I think he carries a joke too far. This is his third duel.

MASHA: Whose third duel?

CHEBUTYKIN: Solyóny's.

MASHA: What about the Baron?

CHEBUTYKIN: What about the Baron?

(Pause.)

MASHA: I'm all confused. All the same, I don't think you should let him. He might hurt the Baron, or even kill him.

CHEBUTYKIN: The Baron's a good man, but one Baron more, one Baron less—what difference does it make? Let 'em fight! It doesn't make any difference.

(Someone shouts in the distance: Yoo-hoo! Hey! Hey!)

That's him. That's Skvortsóv calling. He's the second. He's waiting for me.

ANDREI: In my opinion, duelling, or even being the doctor at one, is immoral.

CHEBUTYKIN: It only looks that way. There's nothing here, we're not here, we don't even exist, it just looks like it. What difference does anything make?

MASHA: You just talk, talk, all day long . . . *(Walks)* You live in a climate like this where it always seems to be about to snow, and still you go on talking. *(Stops)* I won't go into that house, I can't. . . . Tell me when Vershínin gets here . . . *(Walks toward the trees)* The birds are migrating already. *(Looks up)* Swans. Or maybe they're geese. You happy things . . . *(Walks off)*

ANDREI: Our house is emptying out. The officers are going away, you're going away, Irína's getting married. I'll be here all by myself.

CHEBUTYKIN: What about your wife?

(Ferapónt enters with some papers.)

ANDREI: My wife? My wife is . . . my wife. She's honest, she's respectable, well, she's a good woman . . . but somewhere deep down inside her there's something blind and vicious and mean, some kind of animal. Whatever it is, she's not really a human being. I'm telling you this as a friend; you're the only person I could ever say this to. I love Natásha, you know that, but sometimes she disgusts me so much I get sick to my stomach, and I can't understand what it was . . . why I love her. Or why I used to.

CHEBUTYKIN *(Standing)*: My boy, I'm leaving tomorrow, we may never see each other again, so let me give you a little advice, all right? Put on your hat, pick up your stick, and get out of here. Don't look back. And the farther away you get, the better.

(Solyóny and two officers cross the garden upstage; when he sees Chebutýkin he crosses toward him. The officers continue on.)

SOLYONY: Doctor. Time to go. It's already twelve-thirty. *(Greets Andréi)*

CHEBUTYKIN: I'm coming. I'm sick and tired of you people, every one of you. *(To Andréi)* If anybody wants me, Andréi, tell them I'll be right back . . . *(Sighs)* You people . . .

SOLYONY: "Said the dog to the flea, don't jump on me." *(Begins to walk off with him)* What's the matter with you, old man?

CHEBUTYKIN: Leave me alone!

SOLYONY: Not feeling well?

CHEBUTYKIN: You go to hell!

SOLYONY: No need to get upset, I'm just going to have a little fun with him. All I want to do is wing him like a woodcock. *(Takes out his cologne bottle and rubs some on his hands)* That makes a whole bottle today, and they still smell. My hands smell like a corpse. *(Pause)* Right. . . . How does Lérmontov's poem go? "But every rebel seeks a storm, as if a storm will bring him peace . . ."

CHEBUTYKIN: Yeah, sure. "Said the dog to the flea, don't jump on me."

(He exits with Solyóny. Shouts in the distance: Yoo-hoo! Hey! Hey!)

FERAPONT: Papers to sign . . .

ANDREI *(Irritated)*: Leave me alone! For godssakes leave me alone! *(Pushes off the baby carriage)*

FERAPONT: You got papers, you gotta get 'em signed.

(He goes off after Andréi. Enter Irina, and Túzenbach wearing a straw hat. Kulýgin crosses the garden, shouting "Másha! Yoo-hoo!")

TUZENBACH: He must be the only man in town who's glad the soldiers are going.

IRINA: You're probably right. *(Pause)* Our town is emptying out.

TUZENBACH: Listen, dear, I'll be back in a few minutes.

IRINA: Where are you going?

TUZENBACH: I have to go and . . . I promised them I'd see them off.

IRINA: That's not true. Nikolai, why are you acting so funny today? *(Pause)* What happened yesterday by the theatre?

TUZENBACH *(An impatient gesture)*: I'll be back in an hour. *(Kisses her hand)* My beloved . . . *(Looks directly at her)* I have loved you for five years, and I still can't get used to the fact, you seem more and more beautiful to me. You have such wonderful hair! Such eyes! Tomorrow I'll take you away from here, we'll work, we'll be rich, my dreams will all come true. You'll be happy. There's just one thing wrong: you don't love me.

IRINA: I can't. I'll be your wife, I'll . . . I'll do what I'm supposed to do, I'll be faithful, but I don't love you, I'm sorry. *(Cries)* I've never been in love. I used to dream about love, I used to dream about it all the time, but now my soul is like a piano that's been locked up and the key's lost. *(Pause)* You look so upset.

TUZENBACH: I didn't get much sleep last night. I've never been frightened in my life. I've never been afraid of anything, yet now I can't sleep—I'm tormented by the thought of that lost key. Say something. *(Pause)* Say something to me . . .

IRINA: What? It's so quiet here; these old trees just stand in the silence. *(Leans her head on his breast)*

TUZENBACH: Say something to me . . .

IRINA: What do you want me to say? What?

TUZENBACH: Anything . . .

IRINA: Oh, stop it! Stop it!

(Pause.)

TUZENBACH: It's funny how the stupidest little things in life can seem so important, all of a sudden and for no reason. Oh let's not talk about it! I feel happy. It's almost as if I were seeing these trees for the first time in my life, they all seem to be looking at me and waiting for something. What beautiful trees they are! And how beautiful the life around them ought to be.

(Shouts in the distance: Yoo-hoo! Hey! Hey!)

I must go, I'll be late. This tree is dead, but it still moves in the wind with the others. I feel like that, if I die, I mean, I'll still be part of life somehow. . . . Goodbye, my darling. *(Kisses her hand)* Those papers you gave me are on my desk, under the calendar.

IRINA: I'm coming with you.

TUZENBACH *(Worried)*: No, no! *(Walks off quickly, but stops near the trees)* Irína!

IRINA: What?

TUZENBACH *(Not knowing what to say)*: I didn't have any coffee this morning. Ask them to fix me some, will you?

(Walks off quickly. Irína stands thinking for a moment, then wanders into the garden and sits in a swing. Andréi comes in with the baby carriage, followed by Ferapónt.)

FERAPONT: Andréi Sergéyich, they're not my papers. They're official papers. I didn't write them.

ANDREI: Oh, whatever happened to the past, when I was young and happy and intelligent, when I dreamed wonderful dreams and thought great thoughts, when my life and my future were shining with hope? What happened to it? We barely begin to live and all of a sudden we're old and boring and lazy and useless and unhappy. This town has a hundred thousand people in it and not one of them has ever amounted to a thing. Each one is just like all the others, they eat, drink, sleep, and then they die . . . more of them are born and they eat, drink and sleep too, and then because they're bored they gossip, they drink, they gamble, they sue each other, the wives cheat on the husbands and the husbands lie, they pretend they don't see anything or hear anything, and the children end up just as aimless and dead as their parents . . . *(Angrily, to Ferapónt)* What do you want?

FERAPONT: What? Papers! Gotta get 'em signed.

ANDREI: I'm sick and tired of you.

FERAPONT: Doorman over to the government office was

saying . . . says this winter in Petersburg it got down to two hundred below, he says.

ANDREI: The present is awful, but when I think of the future, I feel better; in the distance a light begins to break, I can see freedom; my children and I will be free from laziness, from drinking too much, from eating too much every Sunday, from too many naps after dinner, from living like insects . . .

FERAPONT: Two thousand people froze, he says. Says people was scared. Or maybe it was Moscow. Can't remember.

ANDREI *(Full of tenderness)*: My dear sisters, my wonderful sisters! *(Almost crying)* Másha, dear Másha . . .

NATASHA *(Yelling at the window)*: Who's making all that noise out there? That you, Andy? You'll wake up little Sophie. *Il ne faut pas faire du bruit, la Sophie est dormée déjà. Vous êtes un ours.* (Gets angry) You want to talk, give the baby carriage to somebody else! Ferapónt, you take that carriage away from him!

FERAPONT: Yes, ma'am. *(Takes the carriage)*

ANDREI *(Embarrassed)*: I'll be quiet.

NATASHA *(Inside, to the baby)*: Bobik! Naughty Bobik! Silly Bobik!

ANDREI: All right, I'll look through them and sign what I have to, and you can take them back to the office.

(He goes into the house, looking through the papers, and Ferapónt wheels the carriage.)

NATASHA *(Inside)*: Bobik, how do you say mama? Oh, sweet thing! And who's that? That's Auntie Ólga! Say hello, Auntie Ólga!

(Street musicians, a man and a girl, come into the yard. They play a violin and harp. Vershínin, Ólga and Anfísa come out on the porch and listen for a while. Irína comes up.)

OLGA: Our yard is like a parade ground, people are always coming and going. Nana, give the musicians some money.

ANFISA *(Giving them some money)*: God bless you, dears.

(The musicians bow and exit.)

Poor people. *(To Irína)* Rinie, hello! Oh, my dear, what a life, what a life! We're at the high school, Ólga and me, in one of the faculty apartments. The Lord is taking care of my old age. I never lived so good, ever. It's a big apartment, rent-free, and I've got a room and a bed of my own! All rent-free! And when I say my prayers and go to sleep at night. . . . My lord! I'm the happiest woman in the world!

VERSHININ *(Looking at his watch)*: Ólga Sergéyevna, we're leaving right away. I have to go. *(Pause)* I wish you all the best, the very best. . . . Where's María Sergéyevna?

IRINA: She's in the garden somewhere. I'll go find her.

VERSHININ: Please. I have to hurry.

ANFISA: I'll go look too. *(Shouts)* Másha! Yoo-hoo!

(She and Irína go off into the garden, calling.)

VERSHININ: Well, everything comes to an end. Now it's time to say goodbye. *(Looks at his watch)* The town gave us a sort of farewell lunch, champagne, the mayor made a speech, and I ate and listened, but my heart was here, I kept thinking of you. *(Looks around the garden)* I'm going to miss this place.

OLGA: Do you think we'll ever see each other again?

VERSHININ: Probably not. *(Pause)* My wife and my two little girls will stay on another month or so; if they need any help, do you think you could . . .

OLGA: Yes, yes. Of course. Don't worry. *(Pause)* Tomorrow there won't be a single military man left in town, it will all be a memory. And of course for us it will be the beginning of a new life . . . *(Pause)* Things never work out the way we want them to. I didn't want to be headmistress, but here I am. Headmistress. And of course I'll never get to Moscow . . .

VERSHININ: Well. . . . Thank you for everything. Forgive me if things were. . . . I talked a lot—too much, I know. Forgive me for that too, and don't think badly of me.

OLGA *(Wiping her eyes)*: Why doesn't that Másha hurry up . . .

VERSHININ: What else can I tell you by way of farewell? Shall we talk a little more? *(Laughs)* Life isn't easy. Sometimes it must seem stupid and hopeless, but we have to remember that it is getting constantly brighter, and better, and I don't think the time is far off when it will be completely bright. *(Looks at his watch)* I've really got to go. Mankind is passionately seeking something, and eventually we'll find it. I just hope we find it soon. *(Pause)* We must find a way to join love of work to love of higher things, mustn't we? *(Looks at his watch)* Well, now I must go . . .

OLGA: Here she comes.

(Enter Másha.)

VERSHININ: I came to say goodbye . . .

(*Ólga moves a little distance away, in order not to hinder their leave-taking.*)

MASHA (*Looking him in the face*): Goodbye . . .

(*A prolonged kiss.*)

OLGA: Now, now, that's enough . . .

(*Másha sobs violently.*)

VERSHININ: Write me . . . don't forget. Let me go, I've got to go. . . . Ólga Sergéyevna, take her, I've got to go . . . I'm late . . . (*Shaken, kisses Ólga's hand, embraces Másha once again and goes away quickly*)

OLGA: Now, now, Másha! Stop, dear . . .

(*Enter Kulýgin.*)

KULYGIN (*Embarrassed*): It's all right, let her cry, it's all right. . . . Másha dearest, my sweet Másha. . . . You're my wife, and I'm happy, no matter what happened. . . . I'm not complaining, I haven't a single reproach to make to you . . . Ólga is my witness. . . . Let's start life over again just the way it was before, I'll never say a single word about this, never . . .

MASHA (*Holding back her sobs*): "Beside the sea there stands a tree, and on that tree a golden chain . . . a golden chain. . . ." I'm going crazy. . . . "Beside the sea . . . a golden chain."

OLGA: Calm down, Másha, calm down. Give her a drink of water.

MASHA: I won't cry anymore.

KULYGIN: She's not going to cry anymore . . . that's good.

(A muffled shot is heard in the distance.)

MASHA: "Beside the sea there stands a tree, and on that tree a golden chain . . . an educated cat . . . a golden tree. . . ." I'm all confused. *(Takes a drink of water)* My life is a disaster . . . I don't need anything anymore. . . . I'm all right now. . . . What difference does it make? What does that mean, "beside the sea. . . ." Why can't I get it out of my head? I'm all confused.

(Irína comes in.)

OLGA: Calm down, Másha. That's a good girl. . . . Let's go lie down.

MASHA *(Angrily)*: I won't go in there. *(Sobs, but stops immediately)* I'm not going into that house . . .

IRINA: Let's sit down together, we don't have to say anything. I'm going away tomorrow, remember.

(Pause.)

KULYGIN: Yesterday I took this away from one of the boys at school. *(Takes out a fake beard and moustache and puts it on)* It looks just like the German teacher. *(Laughs)* Doesn't it? Those boys are so funny.

MASHA: It really does look like your German.

OLGA *(Laughing)*: It really does.

(Másha cries.)

IRINA: Don't, Másha!

KULYGIN: Exactly like him.

(Enter Natásha.)

NATASHA *(To the maid inside the house)*: What? Little
Sophie is in there with Protopópov, so tell Andréi to
take care of Bobik. Such a fuss, having children! *(To
Irína)* You're going away tomorrow, Irína, what a
shame. Why don't you stay a few days longer?

*(She sees Kulýgin and screams; he laughs and takes off the fake
beard)*

Oh, you. . . . You gave me a scare! *(To Irína)* I've
gotten used to having you around, you know that, it
won't be easy seeing you go. I'm having them move
Andréi into your room . . . *and* his violin, he can
screech away in there! And little Sophie gets his
room. She's just the sweetest thing! Such a darlin'
little baby; this morning she looked right at me with
those big eyes of hers and said: "Mama!"

KULYGIN: She is a charming child, I must say.

NATASHA: That means tomorrow I'll be here all by myself.
(Takes a deep breath) First thing I'm going to do is
have them cut down all these old trees, especially that
dead one. It's so ugly and scary, especially after dark.
(To Irína) Sweetie, that belt doesn't do a thing for
you. Not a thing. You need something more stylish,
something with a little color in it. And then I'm
going to have them plant lots and lots of flowers, all
over the place, so it'll smell nice and pretty . . .
(Angrily) Who left this fork out here? *(Goes into the
house, calling to the maid)* I want to know who left this

fork out here! Do you hear me? Shut up when I'm
talking to you!

KULYGIN: She does get mad.

(Music plays, a march: everyone listens.)

OLGA: They're going away.

(Enter Chebutýkin.)

MASHA: Our men. They're going away. Well . . . I hope
they have a pleasant trip. *(To her husband)* Let's go
home. Where's my hat and my coat?

KULYGIN: I took them inside . . . I'll get them right away.
(Goes into the house)

OLGA: Yes, time to go. Now we can all go home.

CHEBUTYKIN: Ólga Sergéyevna!

OLGA: What? *(Pause)* What?

CHEBUTYKIN: Nothing, it's just . . . I don't know how to
tell you . . . *(Whispers in her ear)*

OLGA *(Horrified)*: It's not true!

CHEBUTYKIN: Yes it is. What a mess. I'm all upset, I'm
all worn out. I don't want to talk about it anymore . . . *(Annoyed)* Anyway, what difference does it
make?

MASHA: What happened?

OLGA *(Hugging Irína)*: What a horrible day! Darling, I
don't know how to tell you . . .

IRINA: What? What is it? For godssakes, tell me! *(Cries)*

CHEBUTYKIN: The Baron was killed in the duel.

IRINA: I knew it, I knew it . . .

CHEBUTYKIN *(Sitting on a bench upstage)*: I'm all worn

out . . . *(Takes a newspaper out of his pocket)* Let 'em cry. *(Sings softly)* Tara-ra-boom-der-ay, it's gonna rain today. . . . What difference does it make?

(The three sisters stand close to one another.)

MASHA: Oh, listen to the music! They're going away. One of them has already gone away for good, we're alone, and now we have to start our lives all over again . . . we have to go on living. . . .

IRINA: Someday everyone will know what this was all about, all this suffering, it won't be a mystery anymore, but until then we have to go on living . . . and working, just keep on working. I'll go away tomorrow, by myself. I'll teach school, and devote my whole life to people who need it . . . who may need it. It's autumn, winter will come, the snow will fall, and I will go on working and working.

OLGA: The music sounds so happy, so positive, it makes you want to live. Oh dear God. The day will come when we'll go away forever too, people will forget all about us, they'll forget what we looked like and what our voices sounded like and how many of us there were, but our suffering will turn to joy for the people who live after us, their lives will be happy and peaceful, and they'll remember us kindly and bless us. My dears, my dear sisters, life isn't over yet. We'll go on living. The music sounds so happy, so joyful, it almost seems as if a minute more, and we'd know why we live, why we suffer. If only we knew. If only we knew!

(The music grows softer and softer; Kulýgin, happy, smiling, brings out Másha's hat and coat; Andréi wheels another baby carriage, with Bobik.)

CHEBUTYKIN *(Singing softly)*: Tara-ra-boom-der-ay, it's gonna rain today. *(Reads his newspaper)* What difference does it make? What difference does it make?

OLGA: If only we knew! If only we knew!

CURTAIN

Notes

These notes are meant primarily for actors and directors, in hopes of answering the kinds of textual questions that inevitably arise in rehearsal. I have also tried to explain here certain points where my translation may differ from other versions.

This translation is made from the text with notes and variants as published in volume 13 of A. P. Chekhov, *Polnoe Sobranie sochinenii i pisem v* 34 *tomakh* (Moscow "Nauka," 1978).

Note for character list:

All Russians have a given name and a last name, as Americans do, but they also have, as a kind of middle name, a *patronymic*; that is, a name that incorporates their father's name. Many English names, in fact, were originally patronymics, like Johnson, Williamson, Thomson, Davidson; in the course of time they became family names. But Russians still use the patronymic in both masculine and feminine forms as a fixed part of the name. So, for example, Andrei Sergeyevich Prozorov is Andrei, the son of Sergey Prozorov; his sister is Olga Sergeyevna. Russians who know each other only casually, or who have just been introduced, address and refer to one another by name and patronymic. These names are frequently used in the text of the play, sometimes in a contracted form; i.e., Ivan Romanich instead of Ivan Romanovich. Here is the complete list:

Andréi Sergéyvich Prózorov.
Ólga Sergéyevna.
María Sergéyevna (Másha).
Irína Sergéyevna.
Natálya Ivánovna (Natásha).
Fyódor Ilých Kulýgin.
Alexánder Ignátyevich Vershínin.
Baron Nikolái Lvóvich Túzenbach.
Vassíly Vassílyevich Solyóny.
Iván Románovich Chebutýkin.
Alexéi Petróvich Fedótik.
Vladímir Kárlovich Róhde.

Page 3. Irína's birthday. The Russians traditionally celebrated a name day, the feast of the saint a person is named after. A name-day party is the social equivalent of our birthday party.

Page 8. "A writer named Dobrolyúbov." Nikolái Dobrolyúbov (1836–61) was the chief literary critic of the influential journal *Sovreménnik* (*The Contemporary*). He was read by all progressive thinkers. That Chebutýkin doesn't know what he wrote is a good indication of the doctor's shallowness.

Page 9. "Beside the sea. . . ." Here and throughout the play, Másha quotes the first two lines from *Ruslan and Liudmilla*, a well-known fairy-tale poem by Alexander Púshkin (1799–1837), Russia's most famous poet. On page 26, when the sound of the spinning top makes Másha repeat the lines, I have added the next two lines of the poem, since they explain why the first two stick in her head. Pushkin's poems have always been widely known and memorized, and most educated Russians, hearing the first two lines, would automatically supply the two that follow. The educated cat, going around in circles on a chain, is clearly Másha's image of herself.

Page 10. "Said the dog to the flea, don't jump on me." Solyóny quotes here from a fable by Ivan Krylov. Literally the lines are: "He didn't catch his breath before the bear jumped on him." They rhyme, and the main point here is the rhyme and the appositeness of the sneering retort to Másha. The image of the bear is incidental, although I have heard long discussions of this quote at rehearsals, where the savage Russian bear was taken as a vast symbol for Solyóny and Russian Society. But Chekhov had used this quote before; a character in an earlier story goes around spouting these lines, and about him Chekhov notes: "He had an irritating habit, in the middle of a conversation he would pronounce loudly some phrase or other that had nothing to do with what he was talking about." Chekhov is concerned here with a speech characteristic, not with symbols.

Page 11. "A silver service! How awful!" A Russian tea service consists of an urn designed to keep water hot, called a samovar, a teapot that is kept warm on its top and perhaps a tray. So much "Russianness" is attached to samovars in America that we often miss Chekhov's point: this is the kind of elaborate present offered at bridal showers or silver wedding anniversaries, and it seems especially inappropriate for the doctor to offer it to a young girl. A fancy American silver tea-service—tray, teapot, sugar and creamer—would probably make the point clear for an American audience and save the prop people the job of tracking down a samovar.

Page 14. "In Nóvo-Dévichy cemetery." Nóvo-Dévichy cemetery in Moscow is a famous resting place. Chekhov himself is now buried there.

Page 20. "*Feci quod potui, faciant meliora potentes.*" Kulýgin teaches Latin and quotes it whenever he can. This phrase means "I have done my best; let others do better if they can." "*Mens sana in corpore sano*" means "a healthy mind in a healthy body."

Page 29. "Tonight's carnival. . . ." Mardi gras, just before the beginning of Lent, was celebrated in old Russia as elsewhere with parties and costume parades.

Page 40. "You know what Gogol said: Ladies and gentlemen, life is a bore!" The line is from a Gogol short story with a long name, "The Tale of How Iván Ivánovich Had a Fight with Iván Nikofórovich."

Page 41. "Balzac was married in Berdíchev." Balzac did, in fact, get married in what was then part of the Russian empire.

Page 43. ". . . the Panama scandal. . . ." Baihot, the French Minister of Public Works, was sent to prison in 1893 for accepting a bribe from a group of developers who hoped to build a canal in Panama. On his release in 1898 he published his diary under the title "Notes from a Prison Cell."

Page 44. "*Je vous prie, pardonnez-moi, Marie. . . .*" Natásha says, in rather stilted French, "I beg of you, excuse me, Másha, but your manners are a little unrefined." In her next speech she goes on to say, in even worse French, "It seems my Bobik no longer sleeps . . ."

Page 45. "I am strange, we all are strange! Forget thy wrath, Aléko!" Solyóny quotes correctly from Alexander Griboyédev's play *Woe from Wit*, then makes a garbled reference to Aléko, the hero of Púshkin's poem "Gypsies."

Page 46. "I have the soul of Lérmontov. . . ." The poet Mikhaíl Lérmontov (1814–41) was the great Russian example of the Byronic hero and met his early death in a duel. While this remark might foreshadow the duel in Act Four, it's important to recall Chekhov's remark about these lines: "Solyóny thinks he looks like Lérmontov, but of course he doesn't. It's all in his head."

Page 46. "A meat dish called *chekhartmá*. . . . *Cheremshá* . . . it's a kind of onion." Both Solyóny and Chebutýkin are correct in their use of these Georgian words. *Chekhartmá* is a meat dish and *cheremshá* is a kind of onion.

Page 47. "*Akh, vy seni. . . .*" This is a well-known Russian folk song. The words mean literally, "Oh, my little front porch, my new front porch of maplewood and lattice work . . ." but they're no more significant than "Polly wolly doodle all the day" is in English.

Here's the tune, and a phonetic rendering of the words:

AKH, VEE SAY-NEE, MY-EE SAY-NEE, SAY-NEE NO-VEE-YEH MY-EE, SAY-NEE

NO-VEE-YEH, KLEH-NO-VEE-YEH, REH- SHAW-CHA-TEE- YEH

Page 53. "*O, fallacem hominum spem!*" means "Oh, mistaken hope of men!"

Page 60. "*In vino veritas*" means "There is truth in wine."

Page 62. "Don't you like this little fig I'm giving you. . . ." The doctor sings this line, but the actor will have to make up his own tune. One of the actors at the Moscow Art Theater wrote to Chekhov asking him about this line. Chekhov answered: "Chebutýkin should sing only the words 'Don't you like this little fig I'm giving you.' They're from an operetta I heard a while ago at the Hermitage theatre, I can't remember the name. . . . He shouldn't sing any more than that, otherwise he'll spoil his exit."

Page 63. "*Lyubov vse vozrasty pokorny, yeyo poryvy blagotvorny . . .*" Vershínin sings two lines from Chaikovsky's opera *Eugene Onegin*. They mean literally: "Love is appropriate to any age, its delights are beneficent." They are from the famous aria sung by Prince Gremin in Act Three; any complete recording of the opera has it and it is often included in basso recitals. Here's a transliteration:

"Lyu-*boff* syeh *voz*-ras-tee pa-*kor*-nee, yeh-*yaw* pa-*ree*-vee bla-got-*vor*-nee . . ."

Page 63 . "*Tram-tam-tam* . . ." Olga Knipper, who first played Másha, wrote Chekhov to ask what these lines mean. He wrote back: "Vershínin pronounces the words *tram-tram-tram* as a kind of question and you as a kind of answer, and this seems to you such an original joke that you say your *tram-tram* with a laugh . . . you should say *tram-tram* and start to laugh, but not out loud, just a little, almost to yourself."

Page 66. "*Omnia mea mecum porto*" means "All I own is what I can carry with me."

Page 78. "I won't ever have to hear her play that 'Maiden's Prayer' again. . . ." There are two possibilities for the piece Natásha is playing, both nineteenth-century parlor favorites: "*La Priere d'une Vierge*" by Baranowski, or "*Zyczenie*" (The Maiden's Wish), Opus 74, #1, by Chopin.

Page 82. "But every rebel seeks a storm. . . ." Solyóny recites (he misquotes slightly, as usual) from Lérmontov's famous poem *The Sail*.

Page 86. "*Il ne faut pas faire du bruit, la Sophie est dormée déjà. Vous êtes un ours.*" Again, in Natásha's bad French, "Stop making noise, Sophie is asleep already. You sound like a bear."

PLAYS OF ANTON CHEKHOV

1878 (?)
Platonov (Bezottsovschina)

1885
On the Highway (Na bolshoi doroge)

1887
Swan Song (Lebedinaia pesnia)

1888
The Bear (Medved')
The Proposal (Predlozhenie)

1889
Ivanov
Tatiana Repina
A Tragedian In Spite of Himself (Tragik ponevole)
The Wedding (Svadba)

1890
The Wood Demon (Leshii)

1891
Jubilee (Iubilei)

1895
The Seagull (Chaika)

1896
Uncle Vanya (Diadia Vania)

1900
Three Sisters (Tri sestry)

1902
The Harmful Effects of Tobacco (O vrede tabaka)

1903
The Cherry Orchard (Vishnevii sad)

THE PLAYWRIGHT

ANTON CHEKHOV was born on January 17, 1860, in Taganrog in southern Russia, one of six children. While a medical student, he began to support himself and members of his family by writing short stories and humorous pieces for magazines. He soon acquired a popular reputation and continued to write for the rest of his life while working as a family doctor.

His earliest successful plays were comic one-acts, but he had very little luck with longer plays until Stanislavsky staged *The Seagull* in 1898 at his newly founded Moscow Art Theater. It was an enormous success and made the reputation of the theatre and of Chekhov as a playwright. Chekhov subsequently wrote three more major plays, all staged by Stanislavsky at the Moscow Art Theater: *Uncle Vanya*, which was a reworking of an earlier play called *The Wood Demon*, *Three Sisters* and *The Cherry Orchard*. In 1901 he married Olga Knipper, an actress at the Moscow Art Theater who created the role of Másha. Chekhov died of tuberculosis in 1904, at the age of forty-four.

THE TRANSLATOR

PAUL SCHMIDT is the author of *Meyerhold at Work*, a book about the great Soviet director, and translator of the *Complete Works of Arthur Rimbaud* (Harper & Row) and *The Collected Works of Velimir Khlebnikov* (Harvard University Press). His translation of Khlebnikov's *Zangezi*, directed by Peter Sellars with music by Jon Hassell, was performed in 1987 in the Next Wave Festival at the Brooklyn Academy of Music. With Elizabeth Swados he wrote *The Beautiful Lady*, a musical about Russian poets of the Twenties, which received the Helen Hayes award for 1985. His play *Black Sea Follies*, directed by Stanley Silverman, was produced Off Broadway by Music-Theatre Group and Playwrights Horizons in 1987 and won that year's Kesselring Award. His translation of Genet's play *The Screens*, directed by JoAnne Akalaitis, was produced at the Guthrie Theater in 1989. As an actor he has appeared with various Off-Broadway companies and on national television. He has received a fellowship from the National Endowment for the Arts and holds a doctorate in Russian from Harvard University.